The Forgotten

Bearcats

How Mick Cronin and a band of unsung
players saved Cincinnati basketball

Cover and book layout by Heather Koch

All photos courtesy of the University of Cincinnati Athletic Dept.

ISBN: 9781790483839

DEDICATION

To my dad, who had to drop out of high school after one year to help support his family during the Depression, then served in the Army during World War II to support his country. With minimal education and no lucrative family connection to pave the way for him, he got up every day and went to work so my two brothers and I would have more than he had.

CONTENTS

ACKNOWLEDGMENTS

Thanks to Cincinnati men's basketball coach Mick Cronin for taking the time to share his story with me, and to Maggie McKinley, Executive Senior Associate Director of Athletics, who answered in great detail my questions about the academic situation Cronin inherited when he took over as head coach.

Thanks also to the players and assistant coaches on the 2006-07 team who were willing to share very personal details about their time at Cincinnati; and to former Cincinnati athletic director Mike Thomas, former deputy AD Bob Arkeilpane, and Cory Sims, a student manage on that team.

I received a major assist with this project from my longtime friend and former colleague Jack Brennan, who did an outstanding job editing the book, mixing his insightful observations and suggestions with his unfailing sense of humor.

Thanks to my wife, Rose, who has always supported me in every project I've ever attempted, and to my daughter, Heather, who designed the cover and the inside pages with her usual combination of creativity and patience with my lack of technical expertise in such matters.

Finally, thanks to Cincinnati athletic director Mike Bohn for his generosity in allowing me access to the school's photo files; and to Andre Foushee, the school's men's basketball media contact, who answered any questions I had along the way.

CHAPTER 1

'WE THOUGHT WE WERE GOING TO THE FINAL FOUR'

During the three days before they faced rival Xavier for the first time under new head coach Mick Cronin, the University of Cincinnati Bearcats kept hearing that they couldn't beat the Musketeers. Only three of the Cincinnati players had lined up against Xavier - senior forward Cedric McGowan; Bearcats football player Connor Barwin; and Ron Allen, a former player from a small (NAIA) school in New Orleans.

It was no surprise, then, that the 2006-07 Bearcats were underdogs against an experienced Xavier team that had won five of the last seven games in the heated local rivalry. And most of those were before the Cincinnati program had been decimated by the forced departure of long-time head coach Bob Huggins.

It was also no surprise that the players paid little attention to those warnings. Most of them knew next to nothing about the rivalry. There were seven newcomers on a team that had been hurriedly assembled after Cronin was hired as the head coach on March 24, 2006. They were still pinching themselves over the unexpected good fortune that landed them not only in a Division I college basketball program, but in the Big East Conference, one of the top leagues in the country. A few months earlier, they had been playing either at a junior college or at a prep school before tiny crowds. Now they would be playing on national television before packed houses against some of the best players in the country.

The inexperienced Bearcats had won four of their first five games during that season, the only loss coming at home against Wofford, a low-level mid-major program that finished 10-20. They were still becoming accustomed to playing for the demanding Cronin, but found a way to upset the Musketeers, 67-57, at Fifth Third Arena behind 24 points from freshman guard Deonta Vaughn, leaving them unexpectedly feeling just a bit cocky.

"Once we beat Xavier," said guard Jamual Warren, one of those newcomers, "we thought we were it. We thought we were going to the Final Four."

The well-travelled Warren found himself relishing the unusual feeling of being the center of attention in a city that loved college basketball along with its big-league sports franchises, the Reds and Bengals.

"I'll always remember the way the city was to us," Warren said. "You remember Chris Henry, who was playing for the Bengals? We were out downtown after the game. We're out in the clubs. I got my shirt off. Chris Henry is standing right next to me and he's got his shirt off. He's an NFL player and all the people coming up, they weren't even saying nothing to Chris Henry. They were like, oh, that's Jamual Warren, good game tonight.

"I used to tell my friends this: the only difference between a

John Williamson celebrates the Bearcats' upset victory over Xavier, which turned out

to be the highlight of the season in Mick Cronin's first year as head coach.

Cincinnati basketball player and a Cincinnati Bengals football player is the money. That's the only difference, as far as how people treat you (in Cincinnati). I remember standing next to Chris Henry. He's worth a million dollars. I've got 15 bucks in my pocket with no bank account and we got the same amount of love that they got."

The December win over Xavier turned out to be the highlight of the season. Three days later, the Bearcats lost by 22 points to fourth-ranked Ohio State in Indianapolis. They won only four more games the rest of the season – over North Carolina State, Miami (Ohio), West Virginia and Seton Hall – and finished Cronin's first season with an 11-19 overall record, 2-14 in the Big East. One of their losses was a humbling 88-55 score to 23rd-ranked Memphis, a loss so lopsided that ESPN broke away to show another game after the Bearcats fell behind 54-23 at halftime.

Such dismal seasons don't happen very often in a program that owns two national championships, with six Final Fours and eight Elite Eight appearances. In fact, just two years earlier, Cincinnati had made its 14th straight NCAA Tournament appearance and was considered one of the top programs in the country.

The 19 losses were the most since the 1983-84 team went 3-25 in the first of Tony Yates' six seasons as the head coach. From January 24 through February 24, Cronin's first team lost 10 straight games, the longest losing streak for a Cincinnati men's basketball team since way back in 1924-25, when the Bearcats lost 11 straight on the way to a 5-14 season.

But the players on Cronin's team shouldn't be defined by those 19 losses or the blowouts they endured. Rather, they should be remembered with admiration for giving everything they had under very trying circumstances in a program that was essentially starting over under a 34-year-old Cincinnati native in his first year as the head coach at his alma mater.

Certainly that's how Cronin remembers them now from a more favorable perch, as head coach of a program that has made eight straight NCAA appearances. He's grateful for what those players gave him when he needed to establish a culture of hard work, solid defense and academic success. Most of them played only two years in a Bearcat uniform before moving on to play professionally overseas, but they're proud of the contribution they made, whether Cincinnati fans are aware of it or not.

When I contacted the players for this book they were surprised and grateful that someone was reaching out to hear their stories from that trying first season. I expected them to tell me how miserable that season was for them, but it was just the opposite. Despite their lack of success on the court, they look back on 2006-07 with fondness, some saying that it was the best year of their careers, even one of the best years of their young lives.

"I enjoyed my two years there," said guard Marvin Gentry, who lives in Fort Worth, Texas. "If I could do it all over again, I would do it. The bond I feel with the fans and the reporters and the coaches, it was just a brotherhood. I always wanted to be part of it and I'm proud of it. I still represent the University of Cincinnati down here to this day. I actually have a Cincinnati tattoo. I had a C-paw tattooed. I bleed red and black."

The players are proud of the fact that they were the ones who took those first faltering steps back to national respectability for a Cincinnati program that recovered to win 31 games in 2017-18 – its second straight 30-win season - and was ranked sixth in the final Associated Press Top 25.

"They took a chance when they didn't have to," said Tony Stubblefield, an assistant coach on the 2006-07 team and now an assistant coach at Oregon. "They gave us a chance when they probably could have had some other options and would have been more successful. Those guys were a big part – and still are a big part – of getting that program turned around."

I covered the 2006-07 team as the beat reporter for the Cincinnati Enquirer. I saw first-hand how overmatched they were night after night in the Big East and how hard they competed. I wrote about games in which they just missed pulling off a stunning upset and others in which they were blown out. Years later, after Cronin had the program back on solid footing, I thought back to that team and to those players and wondered what it was like for them to go through such an ordeal, what it means to them now as they look back on it, and what they've done with their lives. That's the genesis of this book.

When I was in Los Angeles in December, 2017 to cover Cincinnati at UCLA, I went to practice the day before the game. Allen, who played on Cronin's first UC team and now lives in Los Angeles, was there to visit with Cronin and associate head coach Larry Davis. When I told him I was thinking about writing this book he wholeheartedly endorsed the idea and promptly gave me his phone number.

The first player I called was Marcus Sikes, now an assistant coach at Trinity Valley College in Texas. Sikes, too, was eager to talk about his time at Cincinnati and helped me locate other players.

I called Gentry next. I reached out to Barwin, tracked down Adam Hrycaniuk in Poland, and even found Timmy Crowell, who left Cincinnati after playing only one season. Before long I had talked to every player except Cedric McGowan, the only starter returning from the 2005-06 season. None of the other players knew how to reach him. I tried to contact him through Facebook and sent him emails to an address that was supplied to me by Terry Nelson in the Cincinnati athletic department. They all went unanswered. After I had accepted the idea that I would have to write the book without him, I emailed him one last time. I told him he was the only player from that team I hadn't talked to and that I really wanted to hear from him. He called the next day and we talked for almost 45 minutes.

This book is a tribute to McGowan and all of the Cincinnati players who did the heavy lifting for those who would follow, each group building on the progress of the one before. Their stories deserve to be told, their contributions remembered. This is also the story of how Cronin returned to his hometown and righted the ship for a once-great program that was in disarray with no guarantee of ever returning to the level of national prominence it had enjoyed for so many years after Huggins had resuscitated it in the late 1980s and early 90s.

CHAPTER 2

DREAM JOB

On the day Huggins was fired as the head men's basketball coach at Cincinnati, Cronin was in his office at Murray State, having recently completed his second year as the Racers' head coach.

"My dad called me and said, 'You ain't going to believe this,' " Cronin recalled. "He said, 'They just cut into a show I'm watching. They fired Huggs.' I said, 'Get out of here.' It took him five minutes to convince me that it was real. I remember me telling him to put the phone next to the TV because I didn't believe him."

It was no joke. The genesis of Huggins' firing occurred 14 months earlier – on June 8, 2004 - when he was arrested in the eastern Cincinnati suburb of Fairfax and charged with driving under the influence at 11:35 p.m. His arrest and subsequent plea of no contest opened the door for university president Nancy Zimpher - who was soon to become public enemy number one in Cincinnati - to shove him out the door.

But it didn't happen right away. Huggins was suspended by the school, but was reinstated in time to coach the 2004-05 season, which turned out to be his last at Cincinnati. His final game as the Bearcats' head coach was a 69-60 loss to Kentucky on March 19, 2005 in the second round of the NCAA Tournament at the RCA Dome in

Indianapolis.

A few months later Huggins tried to get the school to reinstate a contract rollover clause that had been terminated by Zimpher after his no-contest plea. Zimpher, who was troubled by the program's low graduation rate and its players' frequent run-ins with police, refused.

In an August 8, 2005 l

etter to Huggins' lawyer, Richard Katz, UC general counsel Monica Rimai cited "21 of Mr. Huggins' players who had significant encounters with law enforcement" beginning in 1990. She also cited a graduation rate for basketball players of 20 percent, including four of nine reporting years in which the graduation rate was zero.

Not only did Zimpher refuse Huggins' request, she gave him an ultimatum. He could accept a financial settlement to buy out the final two years on his contract or he could accept a job outside the athletic department for the duration of his contract. Either way, Huggins was finished as Cincinnati's head coach.

Huggins' controversial tenure as the Bearcats' head coach ended August 24, 2005 after 16 years with a $3 million settlement.

Andy Kennedy, Huggins' affable associate head coach and recruiting coordinator, was named interim head coach. A loyal Huggins lieutenant, Kennedy led a short-handed team to a 21-13 record and a berth in the National Invitation Tournament quarterfinals. His season as interim head coach ended with a loss at home to South Carolina. By then Cincinnati fans had rallied around Kennedy and strongly urged first-year athletic director Mike Thomas to make him the head coach on a permanent basis. Late in the season, many held up signs at

Cincinnati games in support of Kennedy, who interviewed for the job.

But Thomas hired native son Cronin, who had never played college basketball. Cronin had begun his college coaching career as Huggins' video coordinator in 1996 and worked his way up to assistant coach. He left Cincinnati in 2001 to become the associate head coach at Louisville under Rick Pitino, a move that angered Huggins and Cincinnati fans who didn't like the idea of Cronin going to work for one of the Bearcats' biggest rivals.

Two years later Cronin left Louisville to become the head coach at Murray where he led the Racers to two NCAA Tournament appearances in three years. His final team at Murray finished 24-7 and won the Ohio Valley Conference regular-season and tournament championships. The 14th-seeded Racers then took No. 3 seed North Carolina to the wire before falling, 69-65, in an NCAA Tournament game in Dayton.

One of the hot coaches nationally at the time was Karl Hobbs, who was then at George Washington. Hobbs was on the Bearcats' radar early in the search and was interviewed by Thomas and deputy athletic director Bob Arkeilpane. But the interview didn't go well and Hobbs quickly fell out of contention.

Many Cincinnati fans – along with Kennedy himself – have long contended that he never had a chance to get the job because of his unflinching loyalty to Huggins. But Thomas insists that's not true.

"I looked at Andy as a viable candidate," Thomas said. "I will also tell you that Nancy Zimpher told me she had no issues with Andy Kennedy being the head coach. I just thought Mick had a better plan as to how he could get us there. I was really impressed with him. Who knows? We don't have a crystal ball to know where you'd be today if you had gone down a different path, but I think Mick has done a great job.

"I thought he was a better fit. That doesn't mean that Andy wasn't a fit. If Andy had ended up being the coach, he might have done a great job. I made a different decision that to this day I feel pretty good about."

Against the advice of his friends in coaching, Cronin pursued the job. He was interviewed at a tennis club north of Cincinnati the day after Murray State's loss to North Carolina. At that point, the UC job only remotely resembled the position that had been so attractive for so many years under Huggins. There were severe academic problems that needed to be fixed immediately and since Kennedy had made no attempt to recruit players during his year in charge, the cupboard was practically bare from a talent standpoint.

"Not one person told me to take the job," Cronin said. "It was a start-over. The prevailing thought was that it's a mess there and why do you want to deal with that when you've been to two NCAA tournaments in three years as a head coach? I had been to tournaments in seven years as an assistant coach and I was being contacted for every job that was open. Why would I take the job that was going to be in the worst shape when I took it?"

But that's what he did. He couldn't shake the nagging thought that this might be the only chance he'd ever have to be the head coach at Cincinnati. What if he didn't pursue it, would he spend the rest of his life wondering what could have been?

"It's the job I wanted," Cronin said. "Growing up going to games, to basketball camps, it's your school. It's a double shot for me. Not only is it home, but I went to school here. My dad went to school here. My mom grew up on campus. I rooted for UC passionately my whole life in every sport.

"When you've been away from home for five years – and I lost my mother to cancer nine months before I got the job - you start to realize you're not going to live forever. It's not just a mission to coach basketball wherever. Darlene (Cronin's wife at the time) was pregnant, so now you think about where are you going to raise your daughter? All of that stuff went into it."

If it weren't for his strong emotional ties to Cincinnati - the school and the city - Cronin said, "I wouldn't even have taken the phone call from a job that had as many problems at the time as the Cincinnati job had in the spring of 2006. I would have said, 'You've got to be nuts.' "

Cronin had remained tuned into the program while he was gone and didn't have to do much research about what had transpired since he had left. He knew how upset the fans were and was well aware that some of the program's key boosters had withdrawn their financial support in protest.

He was organized and knowledgeable during his interview, his passion for the school evident as he presented Thomas with a list of available recruits he believed he could land to make the Bearcats competitive immediately in the Big East.

"We were probably together for about four hours," Thomas said.

"We covered a lot of ground, not just the coaching and recruiting pieces, but all the academic pieces and the external pieces that go with being a head coach and how you're going to manage those kind of things.

"He went through recruiting and it was very detailed and he did have a list of people that he had in mind. Certainly he knew the situation. Mick was well-prepared. He was able to answer any topic that we discussed. He was able to go into great depth, including the recruiting piece. The kind of kid he was looking for then is the same kind of kid he looks for now and it's been successful. He had done his homework. He had some good ideas on what he wanted to do."

Thomas probably could have made his life much less complicated if he had chosen Kennedy, which would have calmed the fans and perhaps inspired some of the most alienated among them to return to the fold.

On the court, Kennedy had done well as the interim coach, probably better than anyone expected given the unusual circumstances under which he took over after Huggins' sudden departure. Not only did Cincinnati make it to the NIT quarterfinals, many believed the Bearcats should have been invited to the NCAA Tournament for the 15th straight year.

But Thomas was willing to take the heat for choosing Cronin. Perhaps he also knew that making a clean break with the Huggins era would put him in good graces with Zimpher. But as much as Cronin coveted the job, he hesitated before accepting it.

He called Tom Gregory, a prominent Cincinnati booster and the owner of the Original Montgomery Inn, a popular ribs restaurant in Cincinnati. Gregory was close to Huggins and was crushed when his good friend was forced out. He was one of the most vocal in his protest of the move and publicly proclaimed in the media that he was withdrawing his support of the program.

"I had no intention of going back," Gregory said. "I was hot."

Gregory was so adamant in his protest that when Kennedy called to ask for his support after he had been named interim head coach, he turned him down even though he liked Kennedy as a friend and respected him as a coach. Because of his loyalty to Huggins, he didn't want to be perceived as lending his support to the university in any way. He had made his decision and he was sticking to it.

But when Cronin called, Gregory listened. He and Cronin had known each other for years. He was friends with Cronin's father, Hep, a long-time successful Cincinnati high school coach who worked at River Downs race track on the east side of town during the summer. Gregory was a regular at the track and remembers Mick running around the facility as a kid with his older brother, Dan. He and Mick grew closer while Cronin was working on Huggins' staff.

Cronin was still weighing his desire to be the Cincinnati head coach against the severity of the situation he was walking into. He knew that no matter how hard he worked, he couldn't turn the program around without financial support from outside the university. Not if he was going to compete in a high-profile conference at a school with a comparatively small athletic budget.

"If I can't get (Gregory) back, I'm definitely not going to get people back that don't even know me," Cronin said.

Gregory was coming off the 18th hole at Pinehurst Country Club in North Carolina when his phone rang. He was surprised to see that Cronin was calling.

"I told him, 'I'm going to need you to lead the people back,'" Cronin said. "'If you say you're back, then people will say, 'OK, if Tom's back, Mick must be a good guy.' He was great. I said, 'I'm worried I'll never get the job again.' He said, 'Hey, if you're the coach, I'm back.'"

Before the call, Gregory had no idea the job had been offered to Cronin, but he was happy to hear that it had been.

"I knew how hard he worked," Gregory said. "I've always seen that in him. There's a lot of Huggins in Mick and a lot of Pitino in Mick. That's a pretty good combination. I knew he would work. I knew he was a great recruiter. And I knew he could coach."

Cronin also called Jeff Wyler, an owner of a group of car dealerships in Cincinnati who had long been a supporter of Bearcat athletics. Wyler, who was on the university's board of trustees, told Cronin he would help him get through those first few difficult years when fans were still peeved at Zimpher for running off Huggins. That was all Cronin needed to hear. He was ready to take the plunge.

Cincinnati's announcement of Cronin as the new head coach wasn't handled well. While Thomas was going through the process of selecting Cronin, Mississippi athletic director Pete Boone had his sights on Kennedy to fill the vacant head coaching job at his school.

The Bearcats were forced to play their March 23 NIT game

against South Carolina without starters James White and Jihad Muhammad, who had been suspended for academic reasons. The public didn't know it at the time, but those suspensions were just the tip of the iceberg when it came to the academic mess he inherited.

Kennedy had met with Boone in Cincinnati earlier that day and was all but certain as he walked onto the floor for the South Carolina game that he was about to coach his last game at Cincinnati. As rumors circulated and it became apparent late in the game that the Bearcats were going to lose, the fans at Fifth Third Arena began to chant, "Thank you, Andy!"

As I walked toward the media room after the Bearcats' 65-62 loss I was met at the door by associate athletic director Mike Waddell, who handed me a press release announcing that Cronin would be introduced as the new Cincinnati head coach at a press conference the next day. At about the same time, Kennedy was telling his players in the locker room that he was going to Ole Miss and Cincinnati officials had pulled the plug on Kennedy's final post-game radio show, which set off another firestorm among the fans.

The following day Cronin was introduced at the Kingsgate Marriott Hotel on the Cincinnati campus. During his three years at Murray State, his teams had gone 69-23 with two NCAA Tournament appearances. He was the OVC Coach of the Year in 2006. Cronin, who signed a six-year contract with guaranteed annual income of $750,000, made no attempt to downplay expectations in his opening remarks.

"I want to say to our fans that I am here to win," Cronin

proclaimed. "I am here because of the commitment that has been conveyed to me by Mike Thomas. The commitment to winning and continuing the great tradition we have in men's basketball from the administration has not changed and will not change. I feel this is the number one program in the country. No other college job in my mind is as good as this job."

Mick Cronin proudly displays a Cincinnati jersey at his introductory press conference.

It had been a remarkable journey for Cronin. Playing for his animated father, he had been a bulldog of an all-city point guard at La Salle High School in Cincinnati, where he reflected his father's personality. At 5-foot-7, he was too small to play in Division I, but if it weren't for a major knee injury suffered during his junior year he might have played at a lower collegiate level.

With his playing career over, Cronin became the junior varsity coach at Cincinnati's Woodward High School. During the summers he worked at some of the nation's most prominent camps, making contacts that would serve him well later in his career and no doubt helped him secure his first college job under Huggins.

As a Cincinnati assistant coach, he made his mark as a recruiter, helping to sign guard Steve Logan, who became a first-team All-American, and forward Jason Maxiell, the Detroit Pistons' first-round pick in the 2005 NBA draft. When the ambitious Cronin was offered a job as associate head coach under Pitino at Louisville he jumped at the chance. But his ultimate goal was always to return to Cincinnati as the head coach.

He had achieved his goal, but under the most difficult circumstances he could have imagined.

I had known Cronin from his time at Woodward, when he would stop by Huggins' practices from time to time. And I had known his father from when I was covering high schools and he was still a prep coach. I wondered what it would be like to cover a head coach who was 19 years younger than I was. Just before the start of practice in October, we had lunch together at Martino's on Vine St. not far from campus, ironically the same place where Huggins had been drinking the night of his DUI.

Still sporting patches of his short red hair - before opting for his current shaved head look - Cronin detailed how he would handle media access. Unlike Huggins, who in his early days at Cincinnati had allowed virtually unlimited media access to himself and his players every day before practice, Cronin would designate certain days when there would be media access.

Even though we had a previous relationship I still planned to cover his program the way I had under first Tony Yates, then Huggins and then Kennedy, which meant that I would try to be as objective as I could, even though I, too, had grown up in Cincinnati as a UC fan. I told Cronin there would undoubtedly be times when he wouldn't like what I wrote.

He was puzzled. "What could you possible write that would upset me," he said, "if we're winning, our players are graduating and they're not getting in trouble?"

CHAPTER 3

WHO WANTS TO BE A BEARCAT?

At the time of his introductory press conference, Cronin had six scholarship players – McGowan, Devan Downey, Dominic Tilford, DeAndre Coleman, Abdul Herrera and Allen. Within a few weeks Downey announced he was transferring to South Carolina. Tilford and Coleman eventually transferred to South Alabama. And on October 28, four days before the Bearcats' pre-season exhibition game against Northern Kentucky, the 6-foot-10 Herrera, who had been forced to sit out in 2005-06 because the NCAA wouldn't accept all of his high school courses, transferred to USC-Aiken, a D-II school in South Carolina.

That left Cronin with two scholarship players, only one of whom had any meaningful Division I experience.

Cronin had secured his dream job, all right, but before he could do any coaching he had to go out and find some players.

Downey, a flashy point guard, went on to have an outstanding career at South Carolina, where he was a three-time first-team all-Southeastern Conference selection after averaging 11.9 points and 4.3 assists for the Bearcats as a freshman.

"With Tilford and Herrera it was clear that it wasn't going to work," Cronin said. "There was going to be a drastic change in the modus operandi. The transition of our program academically was the hardest part. It just couldn't be like it had been. It couldn't be. The school was too hard. There was no more Evening College, no more University College. This place has become a high-level institution. It had to change. Those two guys struggled with some of the changes, but I gave them the chance."

A week later Cronin made his first radio appearance as Cincinnati's head coach. Appearing on WLW-AM, he talked about what his teams would be like.

"It starts with defense," he said. "In a perfect world, we'll have the athletes to press, a shot blocker to protect the rim and the toughness to rebound it. Offensively, you have to be able to make shots. You have to have at least one guy that can score inside."

Cronin's first coaching staff included Davis, Darren Savino, Chris Goggin, and Matt Grady, who was director of basketball operations. Andre Tate, a former Cincinnati player under Yates and Huggins and the former head coach at Cincinnati State Community College, was the video coordinator.

Davis, a tireless worker and fitness enthusiast with a knack for finding players that others overlooked, was the first to be hired. He gave up a Division I head coaching job at Furman to become Cronin's associate head coach and to help him undertake the massive rebuilding project that lay ahead. It might have looked like a step back career-wise, but Cincinnati paid him more as an assistant coach than Furman made as a head coach.

Besides, Davis was ready for a change.

Cronin and associate head coach Larry Davis, far right, worked tirelessly to recruit Cronin's first class of Bearcats.

"(Furman) didn't want to give me a long-term contract, and I felt like they should," Davis said. "I went to the AD and said I don't need more money, but I want more years on my contract and they just wouldn't do it. They wouldn't do it for anybody."

Davis and Cronin had become friends on the recruiting trail years earlier while Davis was an assistant coach at Ball State and was in Cincinnati to recruit Woodward star Eric Johnson, who ended up going to Louisville. He and Davis hit if off and kept in touch as their coaching careers unfolded.

Goggin, Savino and Grady had worked under Cronin at Murray State, but Savino left Cincinnati after a month to return to his native New Jersey as an assistant coach at Rutgers because he wanted to be close to his mother, who was in poor health.

"It was a really, really difficult decision," said Savino, now Cincinnati's associate head coach. "Me and Mick were friends and I was excited to go to Cincinnati. Then this became available to me. Maybe professionally it wasn't the best career move, but I don't regret it. I got four years where my mom and dad came to every game. It was an hour drive from their house. I'm very thankful that I did that.

"It was difficult to go into Mick's office and tell him after a month that I was leaving to go to Rutgers. I know Mick wasn't happy, but he did handle it really well considering the circumstances. He's staring down the barrel of a gun with what he was taking over and here I am walking in and telling him that I'm leaving. It shows you what kind of guy he is."

Cronin, who had lost his own mother to cancer the year before, understood.

Before he left, Savino was instrumental in recruiting three players on the 2006-07 team – Marvin Gentry and Adam Hyrcaniuk, both of whom he was recruiting for Murray State; and Warren.

"Not a lot of people at that time in April were dying to come and get their head beat in for a couple of years," he said, "so it was difficult. But all Mick cared about was trying to put a team together. He was never going to look at the Big East and say, 'We're going to get killed.' That's not his M.O. We knew it. We all knew it. But you can only control what you can control. You just try to find the best guys you can."

Stubblefield, who had just completed his sixth season as an assistant coach at New Mexico State, took Savino's spot and was a key recruiter for the program until he left to become an assistant coach at Oregon in 2010. Stubblefield was happy at New Mexico State and wasn't looking for another job, but he relished the chance to rebuild the Cincinnati program with his friend Cronin.

"With him being from Cincinnati, I knew that as bad as it looked and as bleak as it was at that time, that he was the guy who could get the program turned," Stubblefield said. "I put all my eggs in the basket of going to the University of Cincinnati and going to work for Mick Cronin, who I had great respect for. We had crossed paths a lot during the recruiting process, being on the road, at high school tournaments during the summertime. We developed a great relationship.

"It was starting the program over basically altogether. You can't sugarcoat it. It was as low as a program could get. We had to sell our vision, the plan that we had for where we were going to take that program. We were selling the strong relationships with the players we were recruiting, that they had a great comfort level with us, that we were going to get this program back on top, back to where Cincinnati used to be. Cincinnati had had a lot of success. Huggs had had great success. So that was still fresh in kids' minds. We sold Mick, our style of play, all those things. You wanted kids that valued their education and wanted to get their degree."

When Stubblefield left, it opened the door for Savino to return to Cincinnati. With his family's blessing, he jumped at the chance. His mother died four years later in October, 2014.

Davis was the last member of Cronin's original staff to leave the program. He announced his retirement on September 13, 2018, a few weeks before the start of practice for the 2018-19 season. On October 25, he pleaded guilty to federal misdemeanor assault charges in Charlotte, North Carolina, stemming from an incident on an airplane in September, 2017.

After Savino's departure, Davis and Cronin did the bulk of the recruiting for that first team.

"I would come in at 8 in the morning or before," Davis said. "Mick and I never left the office until after 12 (midnight) from May to August. You had to keep grinding and checking out every lead and calling to see who was out there to play.

"I knew what I was getting into, but I didn't know how devastating it really was," Davis said.

On some nights, after a long day working the phones, Cronin and Davis would stop at the Frisch's Big Boy on Central Parkway, a couple of miles from campus. As they ate, they talked about how much progress they were making or whom they would call the next day.

"Twice we walked out of there without paying, we were so tired," Davis said. "We just forgot."

Eventually, Cronin worked out a deal with the restaurant manager. He gave him his phone number and told him that if he ever walked out without paying, the manager should give him a call.

Davis was living in the old Vernon Manor hotel near campus. The hotel, which once hosted the Beatles, is now an office building. Cronin was living with his father in suburban Monfort Heights. His wife was still in Murray to sell their house. (They've since divorced.) At the time, Cronin's and Davis' lives basically consisted of hunting for players.

"When I was home during that time, I was watching him," said Hep, who at that time was a scout for the Atlanta Braves. "He'd get dejected when this guy rejected him or that guy rejected him. He finally said, 'Dad, I'm going to have to have intramural tryouts to have a team.' I'm not exaggerating. He would have this cell phone in in this ear, the other one in his hand. He did everything to get players. And Larry Davis was the perfect guy for him because he could find a player under a rock."

They had to work quickly, but they couldn't sign just anyone. Because of the academic sanctions the NCAA had leveled on the program they had to be careful to find players who could not only keep the Bearcats from getting embarrassed in the Big East, but who could do the work in the classroom to lift the program's dismal APR (Academic Progress Rate). They had already been penalized with the loss of one scholarship and if the situation hadn't improved, they could have faced a loss of practice time, and possibly forfeits.

"We had to climb the ladder the whole time knowing that we had to be careful who we signed," Davis said. "You had to get guys that you felt like could get through school. The other thing Mick was charged with was we don't want off-the-court issues."

In simple terms, Cronin's job was to make sure the two problems that had plagued Huggins' program – especially in recent years – were cleaned up.

"We had a deal with the NCAA," Cronin said. "They put us on

probation and there were requirements that our APR had to hit these benchmarks over the next three years or we were getting whacked our original penalties, which could have been disastrous."

Fortunately, they weren't starting from scratch. Cronin had already been recruiting Deonta Vaughn, John Williamson and Marvin Gentry to play for him at Murray.

Vaughn, a guard who became one of the top scorers in school history, was in Cincinnati playing at Harmony Community School because he had failed to qualify academically to play on the Division I level coming out of high school. He was perhaps the one player on the roster who was talented enough to flourish in the Big East. He also had hurt his ankle, which scared off other programs and gave the Bearcats an opening. They needed all the help they could get.

Forward Marcus Sikes, who was playing at Mt. Jacinto College in California, had originally signed with Georgia but was forced to leave after one season because of his own academic problems. Davis knew about him because he had a relationship with his AAU coach.

Warren had bounced around among various prep schools and junior colleges. But Cronin, who knew Warren's AAU coach, decided he was worth the risk because he was running out of chances.

"I knew how bad he wanted to play," Cronin said. "All I had to do was tell him if you don't do this, if you don't do what I tell you, if you don't go to class, you're not playing."

Cronin also signed Tim Crowell, a point guard who was a first-team all-conference selection at Midland College in Texas. And he signed two big men from foreign countries that he hoped would enable the

Bearcats to compete right away in the physical Big East.

Adam Hrycaniuk was a 6-foot-10 center from Mysliborz, Poland who was playing at Trinity Valley College in Texas; and Hernol Hall was a 6-foot-10 center from Limon, Costa Rica who was a first-team all-American at Lon Morris College in Texas. Unfortunately, because of NCAA rulings, Hrycaniuk was declared ineligible to play his first year (he did play during his second), and Hall never played for the Bearcats. Those two rulings were devastating to Cronin's plans and set the rebuilding process back several years.

"Without Hernol and Adam playing either together as bigs or at least rotating, I've got 6-8 Marcus Sikes at center," Cronin said. "It moves John to the four. And they have no backups. Hall was Herb Jones. He was 6-foot-10, 250. We wouldn't have had as brutal of a Big East season. If he and Adam had played. Then the guys wouldn't have gotten as beat down as they got. We wouldn't have got as physically run over."

The Herb Jones reference was to the 6-foot-4 junior college forward who signed with Cincinnati during Huggins' second year. Jones, a former juco All-American, averaged 16.1 points in his first season year and 18.1 in his second when he unexpectedly led the Bearcats to the 1992 Final Four.

Cronin signed predominantly junior college players for his first teams for several reasons. One was that they were more physically mature, a requirement for competing in the Big East. Another was that there simply weren't many high school players left who were talented enough to compete successfully on that level.

Also, if they recruited high school players who weren't good enough for the Big East, they would be stuck with them for four years. Junior college players, if they were overmatched, would cycle out of the program in two years. By then Cronin would have another recruiting class with a year of experience under its belt and one more on the way.

"The jucos were older," Cronin said. "Almost all of them graduated and they made us competitive."

"Could we have gotten a more talented player?" Davis asked. "Maybe in a case or two we could have, but it came down to fixing the program in terms of getting the APR straight and trying to build some sort of culture. All we did those first two years was try to get the culture of how hard we were going to play, how hard we were going to work. For the most part, all of those kids were really good kids and they bought in. It was hard on them, really hard on them."

One player who got away, a player who would have made a huge difference in that first year was 7-foot-3 center Hasheem Thabeet, who ended up signing with Connecticut and played three years for the Huskies. As a junior, the native Tanzanian averaged 13.6 points, 10.8 rebounds and blocked 152 shots. In 2009, he was named the Big East Defensive Player of the Year and was co-Big East Player of the Year along with Pitt's DeJaun Blair. He was named a second-team All-American and the National Defensive Player of the Year.

He declared for the NBA draft at the end of that season and was selected by the Memphis Grizzlies with the second overall pick.

"(Thabeet) had visited UConn early and they didn't offer him because he didn't have enough English courses," Cronin said, "so when we got the job I sent Larry to see him in Houston. He said, 'This guy's unbelievable.' I said, 'I know.' Larry advised him that he could sign up online for the two courses he needed. The problem is that we should have signed him first before we told him that. We should have signed him and then if he doesn't make it, fine. Then if he would have made it, we would have had him."

His academic situation wasn't the only thing that made Thabeet hesitant to attend Cincinnati, however. As Davis said, "He kind of wanted to come here, but he came on a visit and we had no players. The kid looked around and said, 'Hey, they ain't got nobody.' And UConn was UConn at the time."

So instead of having the dominant Thabeet on his team as an important building block, Cronin and the Bearcats had to face him three times over the next three years. One of those games was a 96-51 blowout loss in Storrs, Connecticut.

"So many things didn't bounce our way early," Cronin said.

Cronin had one other piece of business to address. He decided to start a men's basketball boosters club to supplement the financial support he received from the athletic department. He needed more money to upgrade the Bearcats' practice gym, renovate the locker room and pay for charter travel, which most, if not all, of the other Big East programs had. Charter travel was a key element in improving the program's academic standing because it would allow players to get back to campus in time to go to class the next day.

But the first meeting of boosters that Cronin convened to begin his Tip-Off Club was almost a disaster.

"During that first meeting, somebody on Huggs' side said something offensive, something pretty aggressive about Nancy Zimpher," Cronin said. "I had other people in that same meeting that were on the Nancy Zimpher side. They were happy there was a change. They didn't like the old program. I walked that tightrope early. I was like the Flying Wallendas.

"Finally another guy stood up and said, 'Look, there's people in this room that have their opinions on all this. But it's all over. We all love Cincinnati basketball. That's why we're here. Mick's job is to build the program back up and obviously he's going to need all of our help, whether you believe X or Y. We all like when the Bearcats win. We'd love to see UC basketball get going again. This guy's going to have a rough time. This is not what he needs. He needs us all to help him.' He stopped the fight. It was getting ready to be bad."

Cronin then explained everything he would need for the Bearcats compete in the Big East and told the boosters that problems went far beyond finding quality players. That's when he detailed the academic quagmire the program was in.

"We had gone into the Big East without a plan," Cronin said. "We didn't have a plan to change the way we travelled. We had no players' lounge. We had no (updated) locker room. The practice gym that was a part of the Lindner Center was just a gym in the basement with grey walls and a blank floor. And you couldn't hear (because of the poor acoustics).

"These people didn't know any of this stuff. I was there to lay it out. Here's what we need to do. It isn't just that there are no players on our team. It's way worse than that. Here's the problem we have with the APR. We've got to take guys that can graduate, all that stuff. And here are our campus issues. I laid it all out because I wanted them to know how big the mountain was."

CHAPTER 4

CLIMBING THE MOUNTAIN

Not all of the Cincinnati players were aware of the academic issues facing the program during their first year at UC. But Sikes certainly was.

He knew he had already squandered one chance to play Division I college basketball at Georgia, and he was determined to waste another one.

"I was aware of it just because of my past," Sikes said. "I didn't go to class, not that I wasn't smart, it was just the bonehead things I chose to do. I was at a high-level school and I let that get to me."

Sikes quickly discovered that skipping class would not be tolerated under the new regime at Cincinnati.

"From the time I stepped on campus, they assigned a guy to me and a couple of other guys to just stay on us about academics," Sikes said. "I had extra hours in study hall. I had to stay longer than the other guys and I hated it. But I knew it was for a good reason. I did the work and I ended up on the Dean's List several times. It paid off for sure. Chances like this don't come around very often, so you've got to seize the opportunity, and I realized it."

In that sense, Sikes was the ideal recruit for a Cincinnati basketball program facing NCAA sanctions for its poor academic results over an extended period of time because he was not only talented enough to play in a major conference, he was also capable of succeeding academically. And he needed Cincinnati as much as the school needed him.

The NCAA adopted the APR in 2003-04 to measure the academic progress of student-athletes. The timing was unfortunate for the Bearcats. In 2005-06, the year before Cronin was hired, the Cincinnati men's basketball program ranked among the bottom 10 percent in the country in academic performance, with an APR of 756. A 925 was the minimum requirement to avoid penalties and to maintain post-season eligibility.

In 2003-04, Cincinnati had a 916. In 2004-05, it had fallen to 826, followed by 756 the next year, putting its three-year average – which determines post-season eligibility – at a dismal 830.

"The philosophy prior to the implementation of the APR was that as long as these guys were able to be on the court, there was a sense that, well, I don't really care what's happening in-between," said Maggie McKinley, who was then Cincinnati's Director of Compliance and Student Services. She's now Executive Senior Associate Director of Athletics and the department's senior woman administrator. "Guys would leave. OK, well, no big deal. We'll just go out and recruit someone to replace them."

The problem was that every time a player was not in good academic standing when he left it damaged the Bearcats' APR.

At the time, Cincinnati was on the quarter system, which served to hide the severity of the problem from the public. According to

Marcus Sikes, who started his career at Georgia, was the ideal recruit for Cincinnati because he had played in a major conference and because of his renewed academic motivation after he had washed out with the Bulldogs.

NCAA rules at the time, if a player was eligible to play during the winter quarter, he was eligible to play in the NCAA Tournament, even when it spilled into the spring quarter. That protection came to an end with the implementation of an NCAA rules change for the 2005-06 season that no longer permitted a player to remain eligible for the duration of the NCAA Tournament simply because he was eligible when play began. The Bearcats did not play in the NCAA Tournament that year, but did play in the NIT and won their first two games, sending them into the quarterfinals, which were played after Spring quarter had started. By then White and Muhammad were academically ineligible and were forced to sit out the game against South Carolina, which the Bearcats lost. A victory in that game would have sent them to New York to play in the semifinals.

To buy time with the NCAA as it attempted to clean up its academic mess, Cincinnati requested and was granted a penalty waiver two years in a row. The key to securing the waivers was the presence of Cronin as the new head coach.

"The waiver request was based on, 'We've got a new head coach, a new philosophy, and the new coach believes in graduating his players,' " McKinley said. "We put an academic improvement plan together. We talked about hiring practices, his staffing, what their responsibilities were going to be, the recruiting process, (the players) that we would bring in."

The school submitted two 10-page plans which McKinley put together with input from Cronin, one for 2006-07 and one for 2007-08. Cincinnati also decided to accept a one-scholarship reduction penalty during Cronin's first year, figuring that given the situation the program was in, with so few quality players available at such a late date, it probably wasn't going to use all of its available scholarships anyway. It was better to take the penalty now and get it out of the way, clearing space for a full allotment of 13 scholarship players in Cronin's second year.

Compliance director Maggie McKinley guided Cronin through the Bearcats' academic issues with the NCAA.

That decision was not made public until several years later. At the time, it was presented simply as Cronin's choice not to use all of his scholarships, something that even programs in good academic standing sometimes do for various reasons.

Cincinnati's plan for fixing its academic woes put much of the onus on Cronin, not only to find players like Sikes who were serious about getting an education, but also to establish a working relationship between the faculty and the basketball program, a relationship that had been badly fractured during the last few years of Huggins' tenure.

"He had to bring in guys that were academically prepared and that were bought into what we were going to do," McKinley said. "Mick's history as a head coach was that he graduated his players. That was very important to him. And it was very important to him to have his players have good relationships with the faculty on this campus. He knew more than anyone what the previous perception was among the faculty. So he brought in guys from junior college that were willing to put in the work in the classroom and get over the finish line."

There was little margin for error when it came to recruiting, at least from an academic standpoint. In those early years, Cincinnati might have been able to recover from recruiting a player who didn't measure up athletically, but couldn't afford to have players who didn't measure up academically.

"It was a matter of you had to try to find the best player you could," Davis said, "a kid you could get, and a kid who could graduate or you couldn't take him. Because if you took those kids and they bombed out, then we were in danger of being put on probation and being out of the tournament. Part of the job when (Cronin) got hired was to fix it all."

It wasn't like the Bearcats were going to earn a bid to the NCAA Tournament anyway during Cronin's first few years. They didn't have the talent to even consider such an objective realistic. But the academic piece was a matter of the highest priority for the administration, which didn't want that albatross bringing down the rest of the university at a time when Zimpher was determined to raise its academic profile.

Shortly after he was hired, Cronin was required to attend meetings about the university's new academic standards.

"Expectation levels all over campus were raised academically," Cronin said, "which is what Nancy Zimpher's administration was hired to do. My first summer it was like a meet-and-greet with the faculty. What happened back in that era was that it was declared a new day. When I look back, I think the meetings were more for them to tell me it's a new day, and 'You'd better understand that this is serious.' "

Not only was Cronin trying to make sure men's basketball was getting with the academic program, he also was trying to satisfy the NCAA by making good on the promises the school had made in an attempt to ease the penalties that could have been levied.

"They basically said, 'OK, we'll give you a year and see how you do," Cronin said. "They basically put us on probation and said, 'Implement your plan and show us.' It was if all these things don't happen they're going to go back and impose the penalties they could have imposed – loss of practice time, loss of more scholarships, loss of non-conference games."

It fell to Cronin to make the right choices as he and Davis scrambled to fill their roster. That doesn't leave a lot of time for background checks and determining a player's academic potential, so in some instances they had to roll the dice. But in most cases Cronin was fairly sure of the academic abilities of the players he signed.

"Well, it's not like I had a lot of choices," Cronin said. "How many guys are available in April and May in the recruiting process? But I knew Adam Hrycaniuk, John Williamson, Marvin Gentry and Marcus Sikes. I knew all those guys would graduate, just by how many credits transferred and the type of students they were.   "They never missed a class. They had zero disciplinary issues. The stereotype of the junior college guys, it's not always true. Sikes was a non-fit with Dennis Felton, who was the Georgia coach at the time, so he ended up playing at a junior college for a good friend of mine, Patrick Springer at Mt. San Jacinto. If he says this guy can do the work, he'll graduate. Adam is a straight A student. He just spoke broken English."

Cronin acknowledged that he did take a chance on Warren, but did so because he badly needed a point guard with toughness. He knew it would be a struggle for Warren to graduate and he was right. Among the players on that team who completed their eligibility at Cincinnati, Warren is one of only two who have not graduated. The other is Vaughn. Barwin, an NFL player who played two years of basketball with the Bearcats, graduated with a degree in history in the spring of 2018.

But the rest of those players did what they had to do to begin to fix the APR and make a better future for themselves. Credit Cronin and Davis for finding the right players, but it was the players themselves who did the work to return the program to solid academic footing.

It also helped that Cronin convinced several former players to finish their degrees. Chadd Moore, Eric Hicks, Melvin Levett, Nick Williams and Corie Blount all returned to graduate. The combination of those players' determination to finish their education and the new players doing what was expected of them allowed the school to make quick progress in turning around a bad situation.

After Cronin's first season as head coach, the APR had risen to 977. In his second year it was a perfect 1,000.

"He had a lot to overcome." McKinley said. "When we did the historical waiver we actually had a professor write a letter of support saying that the academic culture of the team had shifted dramatically."

McKinley said this was one instance where it helped that there were so many new players.

"There was no one to tell the new guys coming in that this is how we do it here: We don't go to class. We don't care. You didn't have that," McKinley said. "You had (seven) new guys coming in who were told how it was at the University of Cincinnati from the head coach and not the guys in the locker room.

"I really believe that Mick was the hire we needed. He was the right guy at the right time. He was able to navigate through a very adverse situation and get the players on board to help dig us out of the two holes we were in – academic and athletic."

Some fans were aware of how serious the situation was, but for the most part the details were hidden from the public out of concern that if they were revealed they could have further alienated an already angry fan base.

Because Huggins fans still controlled much of the narrative, UC officials feared his supporters would say the academic problems weren't his fault or that the school should have done more to support him in that area.

With the program now winning consistently while also maintaining a high graduation rate, this might seem like so much ancient history. It might even seem as if it were just a matter of time before things got straightened out regardless of who the head coach was. But there was no blueprint for what Cronin did to make things right. He was in uncharted territory.

Remember, too, that Cronin wasn't very popular among Cincinnati fans during those first few years when the Bearcats were struggling to win in the Big East. One fan emailed me at the Enquirer and urged me to write negative stories about him so he would get fired. But Thomas had wisely granted Cronin's request for a six-year contract, so it would have been extremely costly to fire him.

"I told Mike, look, it's a double rebuilding," Cronin said. "We've got to get the APR settled and get guys graduated, then we can bring in freshmen. But we're not going to win in this league until they're juniors."

The players took care of business in the classroom while helping to establish the culture on the court that still underpins the Cincinnati program today. They went 2-14 in the Big East, 0-8 on the road, and most of those losses were by 10 points or more. But they lost by only one at Syracuse and Providence, and by four at Rutgers.

Even after they got blown out, they were back at practice the next day determined to get better and looking forward to winning the next game. They never quit on the season.

"They were great ambassadors," McKinley said. "They played out of their minds. They allowed some credibility to come back to the program so that Mick could go out there and recruit for the future."

CHAPTER 5

NCAA 2, BEARCATS 0

The first inkling Cincinnati officials had that Polish center Adam Hrycaniuk's eligibility might be in jeopardy occurred while he was being recruited out of Trinity Valley, when he was asked to fill out a form listing all the teams he had previously played for.

The roster of Spojnia Stargard, one of the Hrycaniuk's teams in Poland, included the name of Shawn Respert, a former Michigan State star who was then playing professionally overseas. When McKinley saw Respert's name on the roster, she sensed that Hrycaniuk might have an issue. Surely Respert wouldn't be playing in Poland without getting paid.

Upon further investigation, she learned that Hrycaniuk had been moved up to the senior level team, where some players were paid, because he had turned 19 and was no longer eligible to play on the junior level team.

Hrycaniuk was not getting paid because he wanted to maintain his amateur status to keep his options open for college basketball in the United States. But in the eyes of the NCAA the fact that he played on a team where others were getting paid made him a professional.

Cronin continued to recruit Hrycaniuk because he needed big men to give his team a chance to compete in the Big East and because he hoped the NCAA might eventually rule in Hrycaniuk's favor after considering the circumstances.

"We need as much athleticism and toughness as we can get so we can compete physically," Cronin said when the Bearcats announced in late August, 2006 that they had signed Hrycaniuk. "Then you've got a chance. That's why Hrycaniuk is an important piece of the puzzle."

Hrycaniuk wasn't the only big man from a foreign country that Cronin was counting on. He had also signed junior college All-American Hernol Hall, a 6-foot-10, 245-pound center from Limon, Costa Rica. But Hall was also declared ineligible by the NCAA and never played for the Bearcats. Those two decisions were major setbacks for Cronin as he sought to minimize the time it would take to rebuild the program.

"Hall was a game-changer," Cronin said.

Cincinnati officials didn't give up without a fight, filing appeals for both players. In Hrycaniuk's case, they figured that even if they lost the appeal, which would make him ineligible his first year, it would still be worthwhile to have him for the following year.

"It would have been a lot easier (with Hall and Hrycaniuk)," Williamson said. "Adam was a typical European big guy who could step out and had a touch. And Hernol, he was a bruiser. He was strong as an ox, athletic. He reminds me of Joel Embiid (of the Philadelphia 76ers). He walks like him and everything."

———— ADAM HRYCANIUK ————
Center, Mysliborz, Poland

'I didn't do anything wrong'

When Hrycaniuk signed, Cronin considered him such a prize that he compared him to former Cincinnati star Bobby Brannen because of his toughness and soft shooting touch. He was one player, Cronin said, who wouldn't have to adjust to the level of physical play in the Big East. Hrycaniuk had averaged 11.8 points, 7.2 rebounds and 2.5 assists during his final junior college season.

The 6-foot-10, 230-pound Hrycaniuk, thousands of miles from home and in a strange country, had no idea there would be an issue with the NCAA when he decided to attend Cincinnati.

"I felt comfortable because some other college teams were recruiting me," Hrycaniuk said. "I thought, OK, these other schools are recruiting me. They know my past. I felt comfortable because I didn't do anything wrong.

"The system of school in Europe is a little bit different. If (the NCAA) put more work to that and checked to see the system over here in Europe they would understand that that was the only chance for me to stay in basketball shape and not have two years away from basketball. What I did was the only way to keep playing basketball and keep fulfilling my dreams. Unfortunately, I got punished for this."

Hrycaniuk was compensated when playing for the team in question, but it was expense money – transportation to and from games, lodging and meals associated with games and practices, for which he received $976.86 during the 2002-03 and 2003-04 seasons. He then played in the U.S. in junior college for two years before signing with the Bearcats.

According to McKinley, the NCAA rule that tripped up

Hrycaniuk had taken effect in 2002. It has since been amended. In other words, if Hrycaniuk were being recruited to play at Cincinnati today under the same circumstances, he wouldn't have an issue.

The NCAA declared Adam Hrycaniuk ineligible for the 2006-07 season.

In their appeal, the Bearcats claimed mitigating circumstances in an attempt to have the penalty reduced, hoping the NCAA would declare Hrycaniuk ineligible for only non-conference games. Cincinnati officials pointed out that Hrycaniuk was not recruited by any NCAA members coming out of high school and that Trinity Valley, the junior college he played for, advised him that he would have no problem with his eligibility. Trinity Valley coach Dave Campbell wrote a letter to the NCAA to explain the situation, and Hrycaniuk participated in a teleconference with the NCAA to plead his case.

"We talked about the fact that everyone who was advising him was advising him incorrectly," McKinley said. "It's not his fault. He followed everything to a tee. The problem is that he got caught up in a rule change during essentially his fourth year of high school. We were trying to argue that it was reasonable for him to believe that he was following the NCAA rule because everyone he talked to that should have had knowledge of it was telling him that what you're doing is right."

The NCAA rejected the appeal.

"The committee attempted to find an avenue for relief," an NCAA official said in a statement. "But after careful consideration, given the student-athlete's action of participation on a professional team, the standard guideline was applied."

On December 5, after the season started, Hrycaniuk was declared ineligible for his junior season, leaving him with one year remaining. The ruling came less than three weeks after Hall lost his appeal.

"The problem was he had no other place to play," Cronin said of Hrycaniuk. "There's no school teams, there's no AAU. You either play for this team or you don't play basketball. He had no other options. We had a pretty compelling argument. The problem was if the NCAA had ruled in his favor totally, then they would have gotten lawsuits. With them, it's all case precedent. They held their line that if you played on a team where other people got paid, you had to sit out a year, no matter the circumstance."

Hrycaniuk wasn't expecting such a severe penalty, but did his best to take it in stride even though he was terribly disappointed. He was still allowed to practice, so he decided he would use practice to improve for the following season.

He could have transferred to a Division II school and played right away, but chose to stay at Cincinnati. He had played at two different junior colleges before becoming a Bearcat and didn't want to move a third time in three years. Plus he was looking forward to playing for Cronin, which he soon found out was no picnic.

"He was a coach who was expecting from all the guys really hard work," Hrycaniuk said, "and that was new for me. He also put a lot of pressure on school. I had before heard stories that the players didn't have to go to school or they skipped school or they didn't get passing grades. When I got there, I felt this pressure from Coach about school and about going to study hall. Outside the court, he was a good guy. You could go to his office and say what you think. But at practice and at games, he could be difficult and a tough guy.

"Maybe this is a common thing in the United States in college basketball, but he invited us a couple of times for a barbecue at his own house. That was really special to me."

Hrycaniuk vividly recalls one game when Cronin was so upset at halftime that he threw a chair against the wall.

"That was a difficult time for us, for the players and the coaches, because we couldn't win many games," Hrycaniuk said. "Sometimes Coach lost his head and it was tough for the players not to be able to compete on the level we wanted in the Big East."

Hall's issue with the NCAA had to do with the timing of his birthday. He originally signed to play at Duquesne, but he was released from that commitment on May 17 and enrolled at Cincinnati less than two months later. The year before, he had played in a Nicaraguan summer league under the name Hernol Gardener. (His full name was Hernol Gardener Hall.)

"It wasn't deceitful," McKinley said. "It's just common in Latin America that you have multiple names. As we were going through the interview process he brought up playing in Nicaragua. This was after he signed."

Hall signed with the Bearcats on July 2, 2006. The next day, a woman named Julie Lyon, who had become Hall's legal guardian when he came to the U.S., sent a fax to Zimpher, Cronin, Thomas and McKinley regarding benefits she said she had given Hall. When Cincinnati officials looked more closely into his past they discovered that those benefits weren't the biggest issue regarding Hall. McKinley was confident that something could have been worked out with the NCAA that would have allowed him to play if he repaid the benefits using a payment plan. But there was no way to get around the age issue with regard to the Nicaraguan summer league.

Under NCAA rules, if a player competed in an organized league after he turned 21, it counted as a year of eligibility. If he also played after his 22nd birthday, it counted as another year. Hall's 22nd birthday was on July 19, after he which he played in three more games in the summer league. When the NCAA factored in the two years Hall had played at Lon Morris, he had used up all four of his years, even though he played in only three games in the Nicaraguan summer league after he turned 22.

"We didn't have a very strong appeal," McKinley said. "We appealed based on the minimum amount of competition, the timing of his birthday being in the middle of the season. Our issue was the way the rule was written, but they were pretty hard-line on that 21st birthday piece."

Hall's appeal was denied in late November. He stayed in school until the end of Fall quarter and was in good academic standing before he left to play professionally in Poland.

Hrycaniuk persevered through Cronin's first season. He practiced with the team and sat on the bench during home games. But he wasn't allowed to travel to road games.

He never did become the player Cronin hoped he would be when he compared him to Brannen. During his senior year he started all 32 games, averaging 6.4 points and 5.3 rebounds. But he shot only 37.3 percent from the field, and repeatedly frustrated fans with his inability to make layups and other close-in shots. Still, with Hrycaniuk on the floor and with the infusion of talent from Cronin's second recruiting class, the Bearcats won two more games overall than they had the previous season. They finished 8-10 in the Big East, an improvement of six wins. They finished 10th out of 16 teams in a league that sent eight teams to the NCAA Tournament.

Hrycaniuk graduated with a Bachelor of Science degree in Criminal Justice in Spring, 2008. He has put together a successful professional career in Europe and played on the Poland national team for nine years. He also played in the Euro League and won four national championships. At the time of our interview, he had one year remaining on his current contract. He and his wife of two years have a baby daughter.

Even with Hrycaniuk, the Bearcats would have had a hard time winning in the Big East in 2006-07. But they might have won more than two conference games. If nothing else, his presence would have eased the burden on Sikes, Williamson and McGowan.

"Had he and Hernol Hall both been eligible," Davis said, "we would probably have had a winning season."

Cronin is convinced the year Hrycaniuk had to sit out had a negative impact on him the following season.

"He was a first-year player in the only year he could play," Cronin said, "so he's missing layups. He looks nervous. I knew he was better than he was playing. He just tried so hard because he knew he only had one year to play."

Despite his unexpected travails during his short time with the Bearcats, Hrycaniuk said ultimately the experience served him well.

"Just practicing with those guys made me better," Hrycaniuk said. "I worked with (strength coach) Dave Andrews really hard in the weight room and then played my senior year in the Big East. When I came over here to Poland the professional basketball was not too much different than when I was there. It taught me how to fight and it helped me a lot.

"The Big East competition was not easy. It was really tough to play against those guys. But at the same time, it was a great experience. I still follow the team, especially at the end of the season. I cheer for the University of Cincinnati always when I can. I feel like I was part of this team, of this program.

"I remember when everyone started from the same point. That was a special time even though the results and our playing wasn't at the highest level. But I kind of feel like we did a lot for that team because we fought as hard as we could. We tried to do the best we could to put this team in a good situation and also not to be embarrassed in the second year like we were in the first."

CHAPTER 6

FALSE START

Before classes began on September 20, 2006, Cronin sent a letter to the parents of his players explaining what he expected from the players and what they could expect from him. It was a straightforward declaration of what he wanted his program to be.

"Two sentences sum it up," Cronin said. "I'm never going to allow our players to do anything that's going to embarrass themselves, their family, the university or our program. They're going to be expected to represent all those groups with integrity and class. I'm going to be their friend, their father and their mentor. I'm always going to defend them publicly. I'm always going to have their back when they're right. I know they're young and I've got to get them through the tough times in their lives when they're transitioning from childhood to being an adult."

Academically, the new players were off to a good start. All but one of the members of Cronin's first team attended summer school and earned a combined grade point average of 2.94. Cronin established a dress code that required players to wear coats and a dress shirt when they travelled (that rule is no longer in place on the Bearcats' charter flights).

If players wanted to wear baseball caps they had to wear them straight, not tilted to the side or backward. If a player violated that rule, the entire team would have to run. And when an injured player sat on the bench during games, if he wasn't in uniform he was expected to dress appropriately, wearing Cincinnati warm-ups.

Cronin said the rules were put in place for the players' benefit, not his.

"I owe that to them because they're the ones who are

Marvin Gentry dribbles away from two NKU defenders. When the Bearcats played the Division II Norse in a pre-season exhibition game, they had more D-I experience than the Bearcats because of several transfers on their roster.

going to be looking for a job some day," he said. "People need to have a certain thought process in their mind when they see a Cincinnati basketball player and I'm going to do everything in my power to make sure it's a positive thought."

When Cincinnati played its first exhibition game against Division II Northern Kentucky on November 1, the Norse actually had more

Division I experience than the Bearcats, with three Division I transfers on their roster. Two of those players had played three years in D-I. Still, the Bearcats rolled to an 87-41 victory.

On the eve of the November 10 regular-season opener against Howard, Cronin said publicly that he hoped fans would give him a chance. Many did. But many others didn't. They let their anger over Huggins' dismissal cloud their judgment and expected immediate results without fully understanding the situation. Even under the best of circumstances it would have been difficult for the Bearcats to step into the Big East and succeed right away.

Feelings were still raw. Huggins had been extremely popular. Not only did he win consistently, the 6-foot-3 veteran coach had a commanding presence as he strutted in front of the Cincinnati bench. He was often a show unto himself when he demonstratively berated his players and screamed at officials. With his diminutive stature, Cronin was unable to match Huggins' entertaining sideline performances. But that's not to say he didn't practice his own version of histrionics.

Cincinnati fans saw Huggins as one of them. They called him Huggs, and everyone in town seemed to have a story about an interaction with him. They loved his defiantly competitive attitude and the bad boy image he projected. They might not have liked it when his players were arrested and they probably would have preferred a higher graduation rate, but they were willing to overlook both as long as the wins kept rolling in.

After home night games, Huggins would often sit in one of the suites that overlooked the court in Fifth Third Arena and guzzle beer with boosters into the wee hours of the morning. Cronin went home after games and didn't drink, except for an occasional glass of wine with dinner.

On a trip to Providence, I was having beers in the hotel bar the night before the game with Josh Katzowitz, the beat reporter from the now-defunct Cincinnati Post. Cronin sat down at our table and ordered a cup of hot tea.

It was all well and good that Cronin was a Cincinnati native and UC graduate, but he wasn't Huggs. Plus, Bearcat fans hadn't forgotten that Cronin had left Cincinnati to work for Pitino at hated rival Louisville.

Only 7,608 fans showed up at 13,176-seat Fifth Third Arena for Cronin's first game, down from the 8,088 who had attended the season opener in 2005-06. And that was down from 10,608 in Huggins' final season. The Bearcats cruised to a 70-39 victory against an overmatched Howard team, getting 18 points from Williamson. Allen scored 10 points, which ended up being his high for the season. Cincinnati shot only 41.2 percent from the field but held Howard to 12 field goals and 21.4 percent shooting.

The Bearcats produced another blowout win in their second game, 67-49, against Tennessee-Martin, getting 23 points from Williamson, who made eight of 11 shots from the field. Sikes had a double-double of 18 points and 10 rebounds. They followed with a 63-51 win over High Point. McGowan recorded a double-double of 13 points and 12 rebounds. Cincinnati was 3-0, posting easy wins against mid-major teams who basically were paid to absorb losses to help their athletic budgets. They were classic "buy" games in the Jim Thorpe Classic.

Of course Cronin and his coaching staff knew those games were not an indication of how things would go when the competition improved in a few weeks. His players probably knew too.

But reality hit sooner than they expected. In game four, the Bearcats were upset, 91-90, by Wofford before 8,785 fans at Fifth Third. They shot 53.1 percent from three-point range (17-for-32) but lost at the free throw line, where they were outscored, 23-5. Wofford made 12 of 24 three-point shots and attempted 29 foul shots to Cincinnati's eight. The Terriers out-rebounded the Bearcats 29-27 and McGowan fouled out with 4:40 left after scoring only eight points.

In his post-game press conference, Cronin said Wofford was the first team the Bearcats had played that was good enough offensively to take advantage of Cincinnati's defensive lapses, of which there were plenty that night. The Bearcats wiped out an 8-point deficit to pull even at 90-90 with 26.7 seconds left on Williamson's layup. Vaughn then fouled Shane Nichols, who made one of two free throws with five seconds remaining. Warren dribbled down the court and passed to Vaughn, whose three-point shot bounced off the rim as time expired.

"It definitely was a reality check," Sikes said. "because it was a home game in front of our fans. Most important, we're playing for our coach as well. We wanted to make Coach Cronin look good. Obviously, dropping one to Wofford at home isn't a good look."

"Wofford made every shot," Cronin said. "We made a lot. It was a great game from a fan standpoint. I took notes that year and I went home and I wrote that this was a really good mid-major game. I had all mid-major players. Deonta was the exception, but he was a baby."

That was the first career start for Vaughn, who scored 33 points while making nine three-pointers, both school records for a freshman. The nine three-pointers are tied for the second-most in school history.

Vaughn started every other game the rest of the season.

"He gave us somebody who could make a basket," Cronin said. "He was a tough kid. He worked really hard. Once he got some success, he put a lot more extra time in. We knew we had to turn him into who we turned him into to have a chance. Larry (Davis) had him in the gym before practice every day."

———— DEONTA VAUGHN ————
Guard, Indianapolis, Indiana

'Everything was clicking for me'

During his first three games as a Bearcat, Vaughn scored a total of 18 points while averaging 24 minutes and was one-for-8 from three-point range. He started against Wofford only because Warren was being disciplined by Cronin.

"I think he overslept a morning practice," Vaughn said. "That opened the door for me to start that night. I've thanked Jamual for a long time for that. That was my breakout game to let everybody know that I was serious and everybody was going to have to look out for me.

"(After that) the offense ran through me. It was a lot of responsibility for a freshman, but after getting my feet wet and getting used to it, I wasn't going to look back. I wanted to be one of the best players to ever put a jersey on at Cincinnati.

"I just looked at it like my future was bright. Everything was clicking for me. The lights were on. Coach Cronin believed in me. I felt like, OK, I got myself a team again. Hopefully I can do something for the team. If we don't get any better, we're still going to make progress to get better next year. And I think that's what we did."

After the 33-three-point game, the 6-foot-1, 200-pound Vaughn reeled off games of 19, 17, 16, 17, and 24 points. He was held to five points the next game, but followed with a 25-point performance against North Carolina State, which raised his season average to 16.3.

"He was a baller," Barwin said. "He was young and what you'd think from an 18-year-old kid. But he was super-talented and fun to watch. He took advantage of the situation and became a real scorer."

By the time he had completed his eligibility four years later, Vaughn was the third-leading scorer in Cincinnati history with 1,885 points. He now ranks fourth, having been surpassed by Sean Kilpatrick in 2014. Vaughn still holds the school record for three-point field goals attempted (913) and three-point field goals made (313). He ranks second in assists with 511 to Troy Caupain's 515, fourth in steals with 172 and second in minutes played.

"He was the life of the party," Sikes said, "the life of the locker room, very talented and headstrong. That was my roommate. We got

Freshman guard Deonta Vaughn, who would become one of the top scorers in Cincinnati history, got his first career start against Wofford in game four.

along well. I loved him as a player. He was fearless. He would let it go. I would say, 'Hey, I was open, man, pass me the ball,' and he would say, 'But I made it, Sikes.' You really can't argue with that.

"Coach gave him the ultimate green light because he was our best player and he was our best chance at winning. If he didn't shoot the ball, I don't think we would have been in as many games as we were in. But at the end of the day he was a freshman, so it was a learning experience for him."

In four years as a starter at Arlington High School in Indianapolis, Vaughn averaged 23.1 points, 5.5 assists and 3.5 steals and was an all-state selection. He verbally committed to Indiana and head coach Mike Davis while he was in high school. When he didn't have the grades to qualify academically to play as a freshman, Davis chose not to offer him a scholarship, and Vaughn enrolled at Harmony Community School in Cincinnati.

Cronin first learned about Vaughn when he was at Murray State and one of his assistant coaches took him to watch Vaughn play in high school.

"I said, 'What the hell are we doing watching this guy?" Cronin said. " 'We ain't getting this guy. This guy's a Big Ten player. Let's go watch somebody else.' "

At Harmony, Vaughn injured an ankle. He put on weight during his recovery and dropped below the recruiting radar. But Cronin remained interested in him for Murray State. During Cronin's first week on the job at Cincinnati, he went to see Vaughn play at Harmony. At the time, Vaughn had scheduled a visit to Oakland

(Mich.), the only other school to recruit him out of prep school.

"He told me that he had been looking at me since I was back at my old high school," Vaughn said. "He said, 'I was at Murray State, but now I've got the head job at Cincinnati and I want you to come along and be one of my main four guys. You'll be the only freshman coming in for me,' which means a lot because not a lot of players can say Mick only recruited one freshman and I was that freshman. So he believed in me. That let me and my family know that Mick was serious about me."

As a youngster, Vaughn saw basketball as a hobby, something to keep him out of trouble. But when the game began to open doors for him he saw that it might provide him with a means to help his family financially.

That was important to him. He grew up surrounded by drugs while living with various relatives and lived in a homeless shelter for about six months when he was nine or 10.

"You just deal with it," Vaughn told me during an interview for a feature story I wrote about him in February of his freshman year. "I just go with the motion."

Because he had played at a Cincinnati prep school, Vaughn was familiar with the turmoil surrounding the Bearcat basketball program. For him, Cincinnati was the ideal situation because he knew he would have a chance to play right away.

"(Cronin) explained the situation," Vaughn said. "He explained that everything was going to be new. He explained that only one or two guys were coming back and they didn't really play a lot of minutes, so you could learn from the situation and help me rebuild the program. I took it from there. I was just looking to help Coach Cronin rebuild the program.

"It was very hard," Vaughn said. "I've always watched the Big East, but I didn't think it would be like that. The game was a lot faster. Once I adapted to it and started to see everything slow in my mind, I caught on very quick."

Vaughn was named to the Big East's all-rookie team but he wanted more. He had been aiming for Rookie of the Year and believed he had a realistic chance to get it, but the award went to Villanova's Scottie Reynolds.

"When I got through my first three or four games, I figured I could get it and that's what I aimed for and that's what I wanted," Vaughn said. "I was kind of disappointed in that. I think it helped me a lot in my four years at Cincinnati, coming in as a player that a lot of people didn't really know. I came in as a three-and-half star player. For me to do a lot of the things that I've done for the school and for myself, I never take that for granted.

"I learned that there's nothing in life that you can say that you can't do," he said. "You just have to learn from that whole situation. You can't do nothing about it, but learn how to fight through adversity, learn how to fight through people that are not cheering you on. You can't worry about who to make happy and who not to make happy. You've just got to live through it. You've got to constantly keep saying that it's going to get better. And every year it got better for us as a team.

"A lot of people were writing and saying after my freshman year that I was looking for another school to go to, that I was going to leave Cincinnati. But I would never leave Cincinnati because what kind of person would I be if I was just thinking about winning for myself? It's not about me. Even though nobody wants to lose, it's not just about yourself in that situation.

"I would have thought I would be walking out on my teammates and Coach Cronin because he gave me the opportunity to come and play for a D-I school. He had put me on the map. I probably could have gone anywhere at that time. Who knows? Maybe it would have been a worse situation. Or you could stay and fight through the adversity and stay in a tough situation.

"Honestly, I don't know how (Cronin) stayed upbeat," Vaughn said. "He's a winner. He wasn't used to losing. They were winning at Murray State. For him, I think it was very tough. I felt like he understood not to expect too much because of our situation. He knew that we played hard and we were doing everything we could as a team to win, but we just couldn't get over the hump. He had two different personalities. On the court, he ain't your friend. Off the court, he's a father figure to you."

Once Vaughn established himself as Cincinnati's go-to offensive player, his teammates had no problem deferring to him, especially with the game on the line.

"Jamual made sure I got the ball every time," Vaughn said. "He'd say, 'Shoot it. I don't care where you shoot it from, Tay, shoot the ball.' That's all I heard. The fans were like that too. And Oscar

(Robertson). I couldn't stop hearing from Oscar every time I touched it. Even if I was at half court, he'd say, 'Shoot the ball.' That's just Oscar.

"Me and John (Williamson), we made a great combo together because John was so athletic. For me, it was a great year. Sometimes I made great decisions, sometimes I made bad decisions. But I learned from every situation."

Vaughn finished his freshman year with an average of 14.5 points. Only Dontonio Wingfield (16.0 points) and Danny Fortson (15.1) had higher scoring averages as a Cincinnati freshman. Vaughn's career high was 36 points against Coastal Carolina on November 16, 2007. He scored 28 in his final game, against Dayton in the National Invitation Tournament.

Since leaving Cincinnati in 2010, Vaughn has played overseas in Poland, France, Hungary Georgia, Cyprus and Ukraine, and plans to play professionally for another season or two. After he retires he wants to start a janitorial business. He's the father of a son and a daughter.

Vaughn follows his former school closely and is proud to have played a major role in putting the program back on sound footing.

"A lot of the players who came after us, they all recognize that I was the face to rebooting the program, to getting it back where it was," he said. "I'm just glad to see that Coach Cronin was able to keep rebuilding and taking it forward to getting the team a lot better."

A relative old-timer now, Vaughn looks at the current Bearcats and realizes they have no idea what it was like for him and his teammates during that first year.

"I would tell them, 'Man, you guys are lucky to be in a great situation now that you don't have to worry about being the only freshman and nobody having any experience,' " he said. "They get to play with players that had experience in a college atmosphere. I would tell them, 'You guys are lucky and blessed because you've got a lot more things, a lot more opportunities than I had when I was there.' "

CHAPTER 7

CROSSTOWN TRICKERY

I f Cincinnati fans had to pick only one game the Bearcats could win in 2006-07, it would have been the Xavier game. When the Cats unexpectedly delivered a victory over the hated Musketeers in the Crosstown Shootout – one of the best rivalries in the country – it easily became the top highlight in a season with precious few to choose from.

Coached by Sean Miller, Xavier was 7-2 and coming off a loss at Creighton. The Musketeers had been ranked No. 24 by the Associated Press before the loss. Cincinnati was 6-2 after it had wiped out a 16-point first-half deficit to defeat Temple, 80-71, in the Lenape Trail Classic in Atlantic City, N.J. Five Bearcats scored in double figures. Sikes and Vaughn led the way with 17 points each. Warren scored 16 and pulled down seven rebounds.

The Temple win came on the heels of a 59-57 home loss to Alabama-Birmingham. The Blazers scored eight points in the final 31 seconds, all by Paul Delaney, who converted a three-point play with seven seconds left to provide the winning margin. Before that, the Bearcats had beaten Central Michigan 60-50 and Oakland 68-61 behind Williamson's career-high 27 points.

In the four days leading up to the December 13 Shootout at Fifth

Third Arena, the Bearcats were peppered with questions about Xavier. Because most of them had never played in the rivalry, they didn't know what to say. They certainly didn't want to get the Xavier players any more fired up than they already were.

Cronin, of course, was well-versed in the ways of the rivalry, both as a fan who grew up in Cincinnati rooting for the Bearcats and as former Cincinnati assistant coach. He knew how much it meant to Bearcat fans, and although in subsequent years he played down its importance at times, he was laser-focused on it as soon as the Temple game ended.

"He never moved on that quick from a game ever before," Barwin said. "He got right into talking about the Xavier game coming up, making it such a big deal to make sure we understood how big of a rivalry this was for him and for Cincinnati. I'll never forget that."

The Musketeers lacked a dominant low-post presence, so they were a good match-up for Cincinnati. But they did have Stanley Burrell, a 6-foot-3 junior guard who had torched the Bearcats with 20 points the previous season in Xavier's 73-71 overtime victory at XU's Cintas Center.

"They shoot it all five positions, which is a problem," Cronin told reporters before the game. "They don't have anybody that you can say, 'OK, we're not guarding him.' "

That was pure gamesmanship on the part of Cronin. In fact, his entire game plan was based on the premise that Xavier did have one player the Bearcats didn't have to guard.

"Remember Justin Cage?" Cronin said. "Sean was trying to play

The Bearcats ganged up on Xavier's Stanley Burrell in their upset win over the Musketeers.

Cage at the three because they didn't have a small forward. When you're vastly outmanned, sometimes you've just got to take a chance, and we just didn't guard Cage. We took Burrell's right hand away. We didn't let Burrell go right, and whoever was (supposed to be) guarding Cage had one foot in the paint at all times. You have a defensive game plan for every game. Sometimes it works and sometimes it doesn't."

It worked this time. Cage might have surprised Cronin when he scored 14 points and made five of eight shots from the field to tie Josh Duncan as the Musketeers' leading scorers. But the Bearcats shut out Burrell, who missed all 10 of his field goal attempts, including four from beyond the arc. He did have six assists, but the Bearcats had done what they set out to do. They took Burrell out of the game offensively.

Many years later that loss – and his performance - still gnawed at Burrell when I talked to him for my book, "Inside the Crosstown Shootout."

"It was horrendous for me personally, and for the team it was really bad," Burrell told me. "I kept trying to find it, trying to find it, and I never could. They were set up to really take me out of the game the way they were defending me."

Vaughn scored 24 points to lead Cincinnati, with Williamson scoring 18 and Warren adding 12.

"We came in with nothing to lose," Vaughn said. "I think Xavier didn't know how to come against us because we had all new players and they had all experienced players, so it was really tough for them to scout us. But as the years went by, they figured us out.

"That win meant a lot because that's all we heard about for the week and a half or two before the game. You'd see it on campus and you'd hear about it, but you don't really know about it until you actually get into the game."

"I learned so much that week about defensively committing to stopping somebody," Allen said. "That was the highlight of the season. We were all happy in the locker room afterwards. We were looking at the box scores and the stat sheets. Everybody's jumping around. We were excited, not because of the win, but because we as a group accomplished something that we set out to do."

Xavier went on to go 25-9 and won the Atlantic 10 Conference regular-season championship. The Musketeers lost in the semifinals of the Atlantic 10 tournament, but still earned a No. 9 seed in the NCAA

Tournament's South Region. They defeated Brigham Young 79-77 in the first round before losing to Ohio State 78-71 in the second. Xavier's success that season made the Cincinnati victory over the Musketeers even more meaningful and quite a bit sweeter.

"Our former players will tell you that the key to that game was Marcus Sikes' hard foul in the first five minutes," Cronin said. "Somebody was on a breakaway and Sikes laid him out with a hard foul. That set the tone."

Everyone wearing a Cincinnati uniform went home happy that night. So did Cronin, whose first foray in the Shootout as a head coach was successful. But he also knew that tougher times were coming.

"Our kids played out of their minds and our home crowd lifted our energy level," Cronin said. "My problem was that I went home knowing that we rolled the dice and it worked, and that the trickery was going to end at some point."

The Cincinnati players simply wanted to enjoy the moment.

"We came in with a chip on our shoulder," Williamson said after the game. "We knew what we had."

By that point, Cronin and his coaching staff also knew what they had in Williamson. His performance - 18 points and eight rebounds in 37 minutes - was another solid effort from the junior forward. In his first nine games, Williamson averaged 16 points and 8.1 rebounds with two double-doubles.

—— JOHN WILLIAMSON ——
Forward, Columbus, Ohio

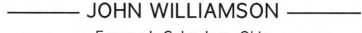

'We appreciated the moment, feeling blessed to have it'

When you grow up in Columbus, everyone assumes you're an Ohio State fan. John Williamson might have been in that category, too, if it weren't for a trip he made with his AAU coach to see a Cincinnati game when he was in the eighth grade. It was the night Steve Logan set the school record for assists in a game, with 16 against Coppin State.

"We went into the locker room," Williamson said. "I remember that like it was yesterday. Ever since then, I was like, man, I want to go to Cincinnati."

But when the time came for him to make a college choice, it wasn't that simple. As Williamson approached his college years the Cincinnati program was in a state of flux because of Huggins' situation. Williamson took the ACT twice and missed passing by a single point, which meant he would have to go to junior college even though he had made the honor roll during his senior year at Columbus' Marion-Franklin High School.

He chose Cincinnati State - just a few miles down the road from the Cincinnati campus – coached by former Bearcat point guard Tate, who would later be hired as video coordinator on Cronin's first staff.

Williamson played so well in his first year at Cincinnati State that Purdue coach Matt Painter tried to get him.

"After my freshman season, he called me while I was standing outside my girlfriend's apartment complex talking to him on the phone and he was asking me if I was going to commit," Williamson said. "I said I wanted to keep my options open and wait and see what happens. I don't want to sign my first year. He was like, well, you might not have the same season that you had this past year. Anything can happen and it might jeopardize your chances of getting picked up.

"He was saying I might not do as good as I did. I called Coach Tate and told him about it. I was kind of upset. Coach Tate was like, you know what that means? You've got to work two or three times harder than you already work. The next year I worked like crazy over that summer and pre-season. My next year I had an awesome season."

As a sophomore, Williamson averaged 27.4 points and 11.7 rebounds and was a first-team junior college All-American. By then, Huggins was the head coach at Kansas State and was recruiting him to play for the Wildcats while Cronin was recruiting him for Murray State.

Williamson was playing in a tournament in Danville, Kentucky, when he got the call from Cronin informing him that the Cincinnati job was officially his.

"He said, 'Watch ESPN tonight,' " Williamson said. "'I'm going to be getting the Cincinnati job and I would love for you to come on board when I do.' I didn't tell him I would. I had so much stuff going on. I had so many coaches calling my phone, and we were trying to win the tournament."

After the tournament, Williamson signed with the Bearcats even though the program was crippled. He verbally committed three days after Cronin's introductory press conference.

"I knew what I was getting into," he said, "but I thought, how many people get to live out goals they put up when they were kids and actually do it? That was my main thing. It would have probably been a better situation for me to go to Purdue. That was the year Carl Landry was leaving, and I could pretty much come in and fill his spot. Purdue was a nice school and I had a good time on my visit. But at the time Cincinnati was the school I really wanted to go to. I decided to just go with my gut."

Williamson was the first player Cronin signed for the Bearcats. If things had worked out the way the Cincinnati coaches hoped they would, he would have been able to play small forward with enough quality players surrounding him that he wouldn't have had to carry as big of a load as he did.

The 6-foot-6, 225-pound Williamson was physically overmatched in just about every Big East game as he manned the power forward position. But he still averaged 13.5 points – second only to Vaughn's 14.5 - and led the Bearcats with 7.3 rebounds per game.

"He was great," Davis said. "He did whatever you asked him to do. He and Sikes bought in, like whatever you ask me to do, I'll do. They were both outmanned."

After the fast start to his first Division I season, Williamson hit a wall as the long Big East season wore on into late January. He scored only three points on zero-for-seven in shooting in 35 minutes on January 27 at Georgetown and was shut out the next game at Louisville, going zero-for-five from the field.

"As the level of competition has increased and the level of intensity has increased as we've gone into Big East play," Cronin said at the time, "he hasn't been able to raise his level of intensity, his level of toughness, his level of competitiveness, and his activity vs. bigger, stronger guys."

In an attempt to get Williamson back on track, Cronin showed him film of Eric Hicks, who had just completed his UC career the year before, having scored 1,231 points for the Bearcats, often against bigger defenders. Hicks was the perfect role model for Williamson because he compensated for a lack of size with a dogged determination and a remarkable level of intensity. Against Marquette he posted a triple-double even though he was playing with a twisted ankle.

Now Cronin was looking for the same determination from Williamson, especially with the Bearcats having lost eight of their last nine games.

"It's a tough spot for John to be in," Cronin continued. "He comes in, and you have success early because you're playing your non-league schedule at home to gain some confidence. It's tough when you're having success and you've never gone through that and then all of a sudden it happens to you. The key is you've got to find a way back out of it."

It turned out Williamson had more of that Eric Hicks drive in him than anyone knew. He responded with 13 points in his next game – a 74-63 loss to St. John's – and 15 in the game after that in another losing cause at Providence. He scored in double figures in every game the rest of the season.

"It definitely was hard for me and all of us," Williamson said. "We were juniors, but we were pretty much first-year players at that level. And the competition in the Big East was ridiculous. You've got all these powerhouses in one conference. But it was fun. It was a great experience because it gave you a chance to see where your skill set was. We lost some tight games. It was just that we didn't have the talent to compete with that conference at that particular time. That was pretty stiff competition for a bunch of rookies who were rebuilding, trying to feel everything out.

"I didn't get discouraged because we had good guys. Everybody worked, from the coaching staff to the players. We grinded it out every single day. It didn't fall our way. We could work hard but if you're undermanned, there really wasn't nothing you could do."

Williamson and Sikes were the two players most impacted when the NCAA declared Hrycaniuk and Hall ineligible. Williamson had been looking forward to playing the three, where he could have flourished with his size for that position, his athleticism and his shooting touch. Instead he was forced to jostle with some of the biggest, strongest – and most talented – players in the country, constantly operating at a disadvantage.

"Coach Cronin came up to me and said, 'We're going to need you down low again and those guys are going to be a few inches taller and bigger,' " Williamson said. "It was like, man, I'm going to have to play that four (power forward) and that five (center)."

But Williamson never complained, not even when Cronin met with him when he was struggling and told him the Bearcats needed more from him. But he didn't minimize the challenge either. At times, he even learned to joke about it.

"When we played Pitt, I was matched up with Aaron Gray," Williamson said. "I was like, Coach, I'm guarding him?"

Gray was a 7-foot, 270-pound behemoth, a third-team Associated Press All-American who was drafted by the NBA Chicago Bulls in the

Williamson scored 13 points against St. John's after Cronin urged him to be more aggressive on offense.

second round that summer. But Williamson outscored Gray, 15-9, and pulled down six rebounds to Gray's 10. Not bad for a player who was giving away six inches and some 45 pounds.

"I thought, OK, he's not going to be able to guard me on the wing," Williamson said. "I'm going to go by him as much as I can."

Still, the Bearcats lost by 16 to the ninth-ranked Panthers, who would advance to the Sweet 16. For Cincinnati, the losses continued to pile up.

"We were kind of shell-shocked," Williamson said, "but we appreciated the moment, just feeling blessed to have it. It was a struggle, a lot of hard work, but that. was the highlight of my career, playing at that level."

Williamson didn't know it then but the experience – as difficult as it was to go through – would benefit him later in both his professional and personal lives, as it has for most of his teammates.

"Once you get overseas and you start playing professionally, compared to what we went through, it seemed so easy, basketball-wise," he said. "Life is a lot harder. You don't know what you're going to be put through, but having that mentality really helped a lot."

Williamson graduated with a Bachelor of Science degree in Criminal Justice in Winter, 2008. He has played professionally in France, Poland, Venezuela, Sweden, Finland, Denmark, Australia, the Philippines and Israel. He said he's probably finished playing professionally at the age of 32, although he was confident he could still go out and score 30 whenever he wanted to. After he suffered a torn meniscus in December, he was ready to move on to a business career in Columbus. He's the father of a baby girl.

"I'm starting on a different avenue, a different phase," he said. "I'm starting up a transportation company here and I do real estate. I have a bus company. We do party busses and shuttles."

It's important to him that all the hard work he and his teammates put in were the start of something good for the Bearcats. "They came a long way, especially coming from a season like we had," he said. "Everybody thought the program was going downhill and now to see us in the tournament pretty much every year, it makes me feel really good."

Chapter 8

RIVALRY? WHAT RIVALRY?

The two greatest moments in Cincinnati basketball history occurred against Ohio State. The first was on March 25, 1961, when the Bearcats upset the top-ranked Buckeyes, 70-65, in overtime to win the national championship in Kansas City. Ohio State, with future Hall of Famers Jerry Lucas and John Havlicek, was the defending national champion and had a 26-0 record after blowing past St. Joseph's, 95-69, to reach the championship game at Kansas City's Municipal Auditorium. Cincinnati was 26-3, ranked No. 2, and had a 21-game winning streak. The following season the Bearcats knocked off Ohio State again to claim their second straight national title with a 71-59 win at Louisville's Freedom Hall.

For 44 years after that, there were no more games between the two biggest schools in the state, two schools separated by roughly 100 miles. It's not that the Bearcats didn't want to play the Buckeyes - they were itching for the chance - but every overture they made to schedule a game against Ohio State was summarily rebuffed.

Cincinnati fans had long assumed that Ohio State refused to play because they were still smarting over the two national championship losses, as if the Buckeyes were figuring they would punish the upstart Bearcats for having the audacity to beat them. Whatever the reason, there was no rematch. The Buckeyes went their way, the Bearcats went theirs.

Then, on November 23, 2005, Cincinnati athletic director Bob Goin announced that the rivalry, such as it was, would be renewed as part of a Wooden Tradition doubleheader at Indianapolis' Conseco Fieldhouse on December 16, 2006.

After the news broke, Ohio State officials initially denied that the game was official, as if such a major development could be officially confirmed only by *The* Ohio State University. A Buckeye spokesman said no contract was in place. Head coach Thad Matta, the head coach at Xavier before he went to Ohio State in 2004, refused to comment. Gene Smith, Ohio State's athletic director, also refused to confirm the game, but told the Columbus Dispatch that if it happened it would not be a one-time occurrence, saying the game could be the start of a home-and-home arrangement between the two schools, with the game possibly moving to other venues within the state in future years.

"This is an opportunity for that ice to start to melt," a hopeful Goin said. "It seems like there's been a thawing in their position."

It all sounded great from Cincinnati's perspective, except for one thing: Ohio State would enter the game with two of the top players in the country in 7-foot center Greg Oden and guard Mike Conley, with a deep supporting cast that would make the Buckeyes national championship contenders. The Cincinnati program was a mess after the rubble left behind by Huggins' dismissal. The Bearcats had very little Division I experience, a new head coach, and they lacked size, all of which added up to a huge mismatch. Oh, and they weren't very talented.

Yes, the Cincinnati-Ohio State rivalry was back on after 44 years, but for the Bearcats timing was everything. And in this case, it couldn't have been worse.

"I wasn't here when the game was scheduled," Cronin said when I interviewed him for this book. "But I can tell you that there was no plan ever of that being a series. I think there was a desire to get Greg Oden and Mike Conley to play in Indianapolis (their hometown) through Ohio State, and somehow we just happened to be the opponent. We were going to be depleted, so I felt like we were being sold out. The game was agreed to after Huggs got fired so our department leader at the time knew that we weren't going to have any players, that we were going to be a bare-boned shell of the former Bearcats, so how were we going to compete?"

Perhaps Cronin never had any hope of the game serving as a springboard to a regularly scheduled series, or perhaps he has just forgotten that he did. Certainly Matta didn't want to play Cincinnati on a regular basis. But it was very much viewed as a realistic possibility by the schools' athletic directors.

And it was very much a topic of conversation among Cincinnati fans and the media, who were eager to pursue that line of questioning when the Bearcats arrived in Indianapolis for the obligatory press conferences the day before the game. Cronin himself was aggressively pushing that agenda with reporters before the game.

"I'd like to play them home-and-home," Cronin said. "Being part of the Wooden Tradition is an honor, but I don't understand why we haven't played in the regular season in 44 years. Being part of

Kentucky-Louisville (as a Louisville assistant), I've seen the national television that game gets. We play Ohio State and immediately it's on CBS. That shows you right there that we should play every year. That helps both programs. It should be played every year, just like Kentucky-Louisville."

Matta was maddeningly coy when he was asked about a future series. "To me there really isn't a rivalry," he said.

Vaughn didn't care all that much about the history between the two schools or about whether a true rivalry existed. He had his own reasons for looking forward to facing the Buckeyes. Not only would he get to play against Oden and Conley, both of whom he had played against in high school when he was at Arlington High School and they were at Lawrence North, he was also getting to play in his hometown.

"I've got a lot of family members coming," he said. "Most people haven't seen me play in a long time at home. I'm looking forward to showing them that I've gotten better and improved my game a whole lot."

A storybook ending would have had the undermanned Bearcats rising from the ashes to knock off Ohio State in a replay of the 1961 and 1962 title games. But there was no way that was going to happen this time. The expected Buckeye blowout unfolded and it was every bit as ugly as Cronin had feared.

Cincinnati hung tough early and trailed by only four points midway through the first half, but the feisty Bearcats' competitiveness didn't last long.

"We came out on fire," Sikes said. "We were ready to play, but their skill level was well above ours. It was just hard to score with Greg Oden in the middle. We couldn't get layups. We couldn't get any shots in the paint against him, and every time they came down they converted.

"I remember one specific play that Deonta called, and J-Will was like, 'Sikes, when you catch it, drop it down to me, I'm going to dunk on Greg Oden. I'm going to get a highlight. We're going to lose, but I'm going to get a highlight.' He dunked, but I think he missed it and went to the free throw line."

There was no stopping the superior Buckeyes, who led 42-14 at halftime, sending reporters on press row paging through the media guide to locate the most lopsided losses in Cincinnati history. As I wrote in the Enquirer for the next day, "In the end, OSU's 72-50 victory was not one for the record books, but it certainly wasn't worth waiting the 44 years that had transpired since the last time the two schools met in 1962."

It was a sobering comeuppance for the Bearcats, who just a few days earlier were giddy as they celebrated their emotional upset victory over crosstown rival Xavier.

Oden scored 14 points and pulled down 11 rebounds in 27 minutes. Conley scored eight points in 25 minutes, and fellow homeboy Vaughn was held to five points on 2-of-11 shooting.

Even though Williamson didn't get the highlight he was seeking it was a special game for him. He had grown up surrounded by OSU fans, and now he had a monster game of 17 points and 16 rebounds against the Buckeyes.

"I had a lot of people watching, so I really wanted to win," Williamson said. "They were loaded. We didn't play well that game at all. I remember Coach coming in and yelling at us. He said something to us at the half like, if I have to bench everybody, I will. He said so many things that were off the wall, I can't even remember all of them. I've been to a few practices since then and he's still the same Mick."

Perhaps the most memorable moment in the game occurred when Barwin was forced to guard Oden. That was a Barwin highlight that he still cherishes.

"I'd love to look at some of those advanced NBA stats like they have now," Barwin said, "because I swear we were like plus-two while I was in the game. I got a rebound over Greg Oden. I think he scored like two points while I was on him, but I got a steal on him when he tried to post me up. It was a lot of fun to go against him because of the hype that was surrounding him that season.

"I just thought to push him away as far away from the basket as I could. That's what I could do to give myself the best chance to defend him. I knew the farther he caught the ball from the rim the better chance I had."

At the time, Barwin was listed at 6-foot-4, 240. Oden was listed at 7-feet, 250 and was one of the most celebrated college players in the country. He was the first player taken in the NBA draft the following June, by the Portland Trail Blazers, but injuries prevented him from having the career that was predicted for him.

Barwin was a sophomore tight end on Cincinnati's football team and a future All-Pro defensive end/linebacker in the NFL. But on this day, he was a little-known football player who was helping his school on the basketball court trying his best to contain the towering Oden by throwing his weight around.

"I don't think he said anything," Barwin said. "I'm sure he was a little confused about what was going on."

Barwin scored two points with three rebounds and committed four fouls in nine minutes.

The game was also memorable for Branden Miller, Cincinnati's walk-on guard who scored a career-high six points against the Buckeyes in eight minutes. He took two shots, both three-pointers, and made them. They were UC's only two three-pointers in 24 attempts.

"The two or three games before I don't think I even got in the game," Miller said. "I went out there and I hit a couple of shots, I got a steal and maybe a rebound. (As a walk-on) everything you do is to try to instill confidence in you with the coaches. He only has 200 minutes to hand out and I'm trying to get a few of them. It was just another opportunity for me to get in there and show what I can do and try to gain some confidence with him. I think I played like the last five minutes.

"I can remember an image of where I was standing in front of our bench when I made those shots. I think they were both on the right side. I had so few buckets in my career that I can remember a lot of them."

Overall, though, the much anticipated match-up against Ohio State was a bust from the Bearcats' perspective. There was almost no way it couldn't have been.

The Buckeyes went on to post a 35-4 record, won the Big Ten championship with a 15-1 record and played in the national championship game, where they lost to Florida 84-75.

All that pre-game talk about the game leading to a recurring series between the two schools amounted to nothing. Matta made that abundantly clear well before tip-off.

"I'm not going to beat a dead horse," Cronin said after the game. "From the comments the last few days it's pretty clear they're not interested. They caught us when we were down. Cincinnati basketball has a great tradition and has been quite successful since 1962, so if they don't want to play us that's fine."

I asked Cronin how he felt about the fact that Ohio State had finally agreed to play Cincinnati when the Bearcats were in such a weakened state.

"I think that's a question you have to ask yourself," he said. "Why did they elect to schedule the game at this time? I know that the overtures have been going on for years. I've made mine. If they don't want to play, that's fine."

Then I asked Matta if Ohio State would have agreed to play the Bearcats if their program weren't so depleted. "I don't know," he said. "I don't even know who scheduled this game. Nobody was feeling sorry for me when I got to Ohio State."

As fate would have it, Cincinnati and Ohio State played again five years later in the Sweet 16 in Boston on March 22, 2012, with Ohio State winning, 81-66. In 2017, Matta was fired and replaced by Chris

Holtmann, the former Butler coach, who agreed to play the Bearcats on November 7, 2018, to help them open newly renovated Fifth Third Arena, with the Bearcats agreeing to play at Ohio State the following season. OSU won that game 64-56, before a sellout crowd of 12,012, spoiling the debut of Cincinnati's new arena. It was to the first meeting between the two schools in Cincinnati since January 3, 1920, when the Buckeyes won 15-13 at Schmidlapp Hall on the Cincinnati campus.

The loss to Ohio State is still mentioned by many of the Cincinnati players as the lowlight of that season.

"I remember getting my ass kicked, and not being able to do nothing about it," said Allen, who played six minutes in that game. "When we played a team like Ohio State we didn't really know what we were getting into. I knew and a few other guys knew. Ced knew. There was just such a disconnect from the younger group to the juco guys and the returners. It was literally like two or three teams in one. It was a mess, man, it was a mess."

"That game really let me know how much work we needed to do," McGowan said, "and how much we were missing those guys who became ineligible because we needed those bodies. That was one of those games that had me after the game kind of questioning, 'What are we doing here?' We need to get our stuff together."

The Bearcats left Conseco Fieldhouse with a 7-3 record and a heavy dose of reality. In the space of three days they had experienced their best moment of the season and their lowest. And they still had 20 games left. They wouldn't play a team as talented as Ohio State the rest of the season, but that was small consolation because they still had the rugged Big East schedule looming and that included two more teams that would be ranked among the nation's Top 15. The grind was just beginning.

"We were just outmanned," Cronin said. "You don't play a Final Four team with a 7-footer, and I've got Marcus Sikes and Connor Barwin. And they had pros on the wings. In those games, there were a lot of times when I felt bad for my guys because I know they were outmanned, and you don't want kids to get embarrassed. I could deal with it. I'm a professional. I get it. That doesn't make the other guy a better coach. He's just got better players. But with kids, you worry that it demoralizes them. So you've got to get them through it and get them to move on. There was a lot of that the entire season."

——— CONNOR BARWIN ———
Forward, Hazel Park, Michigan

'He demanded everything you had'

On a team with so many first-year players, Barwin qualified as a veteran even though he had played only one season and was attending Cincinnati on a football scholarship.

As a freshman on Andy Kennedy's team the year before, Barwin played in 18 games, averaging 9.9 minutes per contest. He scored all of 18 points with 2.2 rebounds per game, making seven of 18 shots from the field and four of five from the line. He also had a great time helping Kennedy's short-handed Bearcats in a pinch, calling it "one of the most fun years I've had in sports."

When Cronin came on board, Barwin didn't know for sure if he would be asked to remain part of the team. He didn't have to wait long to find out his spot was secure.

"I think the way (Cronin) said it was, 'If you want to play, we still need you to play. This is my first year and we're definitely still in transition,' " Barwin said.

"The way I remember it is that we were absolutely terrible that first year. Well, I don't want to say bad, maybe just a little outmatched. We competed. We had a bunch of guys from juco, guys he was recruiting to go to Murray State, so we didn't have a lot of Big East caliber players."

The experience of playing under Cronin was entirely different from Barwin's first year under Kennedy, when the Bearcats had a senior-dominated team. Those players had a strong allegiance to Kennedy and his assistant Frank Martin. And even though they didn't have much depth, their top five or six players were experienced, athletic and talented.

Eric Hicks, James White, Jihad Muhammad, Chadd Moore, and Armein Kirkland all were signed by Huggins and had expected to play their entire college careers for him. Kirkland had issues with Huggins at times, but got along fine with Kennedy. Freshman point guard Devan Downey was added to the mix in 2005. Those players held their own in the Big East with an 8-8 record, and many Cincinnati fans believe they should have been invited to the NCAA Tournament with a 19-12 overall record. Instead, they had to settle for the NIT.

As I covered that team, I could see how those players felt about Kennedy and how badly they wanted him to become the head coach on a permanent basis. It was fun to write about a team that played with such strong motivation.

When Barwin first went out for basketball after Kennedy hung out the Help Wanted sign, the veteran players took him under their wing. They liked how hard he played and how he approached the game with such a physical style. And any time a football player ends up making a meaningful contribution to the basketball team, it's a good story.

When the football team went to the Orange Bowl after Barwin's senior season I did a daily diary with him from Miami in the week leading up to the game. I looked forward to that every day, and I'd like to think he did too. And like his basketball teammates, I got a kick out of watching him lumber fearlessly up and down the court, wearing a headband to contain his long, dark hair.

"We were in every game and we were probably favored to win most of the games we were playing," Barwin said. "We had this us against what was happening to Andy mentality. We were all feeling like he wasn't really getting an opportunity. There was definitely a feeling of we're doing this for Andy. We're going to prove everybody wrong. Andy should get this job and he doesn't have a chance.

"That was one of my favorite teams that I've ever been a part of because I was so young, too. We were winning a lot of games. And then with Mick, it was like everybody knew we were in transition, that this was the start of hopefully a long run (for him), which it turned out

UC football player Connor Barwin was appreciated by his basketball teammates for his physical approach to the game.

to be.

It was a bunch of guys that weren't supposed to be there. We were outmatched every night. I wasn't just the new guy (as he had been the year before). Everybody was kind of new and young. "

Cronin and his coaching staff were happy to have Barwin. He lacked the athleticism of some of the other players, but he made up for it with other qualities.

"We needed bodies and he liked basketball," associate head coach Davis said. "Mick was accommodating to him and he was accommodating to us. He would say I'll be out there as soon as football's over. He helped with the culture. He showed up every day and he battled. He led the way in terms of how hard he practiced every day. And he played hard. All the guys had to fall in line. You had to. Everybody had to. He was a big part of toughness and playing hard."

Barwin was recruited to Cincinnati by football coach Mark Dantonio as a tight end. Brian Kelly moved him to defensive end for his senior year in 2008, and he led the Big East in sacks with 11 and was a first-team all-conference selection. He was drafted in the second round by the NFL's Houston Texans and has flourished as a defensive end and outside linebacker. He recorded 14.5 sacks playing for the Philadelphia Eagles in 2014 and was chosen to play in the Pro Bowl. He has also played for the Los Angeles Rams, and signed a two-year contract with the New York Giants in 2018.

Barwin's sophomore year at Cincinnati was Dantonio's final year as Cincinnati's head football coach. The football Bearcats went 8-5 overall, 4-3 in the Big East in 2006 and defeated Western Michigan 27-24 in the International Bowl in Toronto. After the bowl game, Barwin was all in with the basketball team.

Soon Barwin developed the same level of respect for Cronin that he had for Kennedy, and to this day he remains impressed with the intensity Cronin radiated day in and day out.

"Mick was trying to build a culture, and that's why he was so intense," Barwin said. "I've always admired him for the way he stayed after us that first year. I didn't realize what he was doing until I was older and I could reflect on it after being on a lot more teams. He never really explained that. He demanded everything that you had and probably a little bit more than we all had. That's just the way it was. Every single night, every single practice, just looking back he was trying to create a standard level of play and intensity."

Barwin was popular with his teammates, who appreciated how hard he played and welcomed his football-like physicality.

"He was my roommate on road trips," Sikes said. "He was a tough, physical football guy who could play basketball as well. 'Just use all your fouls, Connor.' That's what we used to tell him. Coach preached toughness anyway, and that's what Connor brought from day one. He was fun to be around. He brought a different dynamic to the team. He blended in well."

Barwin's role was the same under both head coaches.

"I think maybe (Cronin) expected a little bit less out of me because he was depending so much on those other guys who were planning to be there for the next year or two," Barwin said. "He was trying to work on their skill set and their basketball skills moreso than me. (The previous year) I had Andy Kennedy and Frank Martin. Andy Kennedy gave me a pass to do anything. Anything I did was just a bonus. But Frank Martin used to get all over me and yell at me. But my role was pretty the same – play hard, show a little energy when I got in there, be a smart defensive player. That was about it.

"I was much closer with the players on Andy's team because they were mostly all seniors except for maybe one or two juniors. They took me in as the young freshman football player. That second year everybody was new. It wasn't the same relationship. It was everybody's first time playing for Mick, everybody's first or second year at UC."

Barwin doesn't remember much about the non-conference games, but he remembers what it was like in the Big East, "especially those last six weeks when it really got bad for us. Early on, I thought we were going to be better than we were, but I was aware going from playing with Huggins' guys, what it was like with James White and Eric Hicks, to what we were playing with under Mick that first year.

"I wasn't as good as any of them," Barwin said, "but I was still at all those practices and I knew that the level of play was different. You wanted to play as hard as you could for Mick because you saw how much it affected him and how bad he wanted to win."

As he looks back on his college basketball career, Barwin wishes he had given himself more credit for his basketball prowess. At times he thought perhaps he didn't belong on the same floor with such talented athletes, especially during his first season. He played in 23 games during Cronin's first season, averaging 1.2 points and 1.4 rebounds in 10.3 minutes per game. He shot 43.5 percent from the floor and was five-for-13 from the line.

"I liked playing for Mick, and I've seen the success he's had," Barwin said. "But some of my best memories were from that freshman year, playing for Andy Kennedy with those guys in the Big East, playing in a bunch of NBA arenas, playing against Jeff Green and the guys from Syracuse, Georgetown."

Even though his first year of basketball at Cincinnati still ranks as one of his favorite years in all of sports, it was also one of his most disappointing "because that was the year we could have and probably should have gone to the tournament and didn't. I would have loved to experience playing in the NCAA Tournament.

"It wasn't nearly as enjoyable (the next year). Like any athlete, you enjoy winning, and we weren't winning. I look back on it now just thankful to have played for Mick. It was a great example for me as a young person about resilience. I probably didn't realize it (at the time). What we went through always made football seem not as hard. I was loving being there. I never got discouraged. I was just happy to still be playing basketball. If anything, I felt bad for Mick and some of those other guys that were high-caliber basketball players. He definitely got frustrated and pissed off. I was just happy to be part of it, happy to have played for Mick. He's one of the few coaches that I talk to consistently, which is what I love about him."

Barwin makes his off-season home in Philadelphia. He graduated with a Bachelor of Arts degree in History in Spring, 2018. At the time of this writing, he and his wife were expecting their first child.

——— BRANDEN MILLER ———
Guard, Cincinnati, Ohio

'People were protesting. They didn't want to show up.'

In November 2009, early in the first season after Miller completed his eligibility, the Bearcats lost in the championship game of the Maui Invitational, 61-59 in overtime to Gonzaga. To reach that point, they had beaten Vanderbilt and Maryland. After the loss, Cronin sent a text message to the players from his first team.

"He said, 'Hey, I want you guys to know that when we start being successful, this is all for you,' " Miller said. " 'You guys laid the foundation and I want to thank you.' It was pretty cool. It makes you feel like everything we went through it was all for a better cause."

As a walk-on guard out of Indian Hill High School in suburban Cincinnati, Miller was following in a long line of Bearcat walk-ons who became fan favorites, guys like John Meeker, Alex Meacham, and many others. He was surprised when he was asked to walk on by Andy Assaley, who was then video coordinator/program associate in Huggins' final year as head coach.

"He just randomly saw me at a high school game," Miller said. "I think I played pretty well. I think I had a dunk or two and he was like, 'Hey, if you'd like to come and walk on we'd love to have you.' I was expecting to play for Huggins. Then he was fired in August. That's when I was actually worried, like hey, am I still going to have a spot here?"

Having grown up as a Cincinnati fan, Miller had been looking forward to playing for the demanding Huggins.

"I'd be watching games back when they were on FOX every week and I'd see him all pissed off going into halftime or at the end of a game," Miller said. "I liked that about him, always wanting more, never settling. It was just jaw-dropping to everyone (when he was fired)."

Before he ever played in a game for the Bearcats, Miller was thrust into the turmoil surrounding the program, with Kennedy now running the show on an interim basis. He had no illusions about getting a lot of playing time. Miller was just happy to be part of the team he grew up following. Besides, the only schools that had shown an interest in him were from Division III and some from Division II that were interested in having him walk on. Choosing Cincinnati, with a chance to play in the Big East, was an easy decision.

"I would like to think I could play," Miller said. "Our (high school) team did well. I scored like 16 a game. To be able to play at (the college) level you have to be able to check some boxes. You have to be long enough and athletic enough before they can even look at you. You can be skilled and you can be able to score, but if you're not quite athletic enough and not quite tall enough, then you're not going to be able to play at that level."

Miller enjoyed his one season playing under Kennedy, but it took awhile before he felt entirely comfortable with his new teammates, who put him through their own version of initiation.

"There were guys who had been there for four years," Miller said. "That was very intimidating for me to try to fit in and show them that I could compete, that I could play and that I belonged there. It was a whole different world. There were some other freshmen who got it worse than I did. I'm not very combative. I'll just laugh it off. I'm not trying to get in anybody's face and talk trash to anyone. Just let me fit in and let's play basketball. Eric Hicks was the one guy when I was playing that you're really glad he's on your side. He would go to bat for any one of his teammates. He could pick on you all during practice, but if somebody messed with you from outside our little circle, he'd be the first one to defend you."

Miller played in 12 games as a freshman, averaging two minutes, and scoring a total of six points. During that first year, he could sense the lingering anger among the fans even as they rallied around Kennedy as the season unfolded.

"People were protesting," Miller said. "They didn't want to show up. They didn't renew their season tickets. They were all so mad about that Bob Huggins thing that it turned them off, and then attendance started to slip little by little."

It slipped even more at the end of the season when the job went to Cronin instead of Kennedy. Miller noticed the smaller crowds because he knew what attendance had been like during the program's best years under Huggins. But he said it didn't really affect the players on the 2006-07 team because they didn't know any better. By the time they showed up, this was the norm.

"I went from high school to playing in front of 8,000 people," Miller said. "That's a lot of people. It's all relative, I guess."

There was never any doubt that Miller would be asked to return under Cronin, who needed all the players he could find. During his first team meeting, he said he wanted all of them to return. But when the smoke had cleared, the only players who came back were McGowan, Allen, Barwin and Miller.

Not surprisingly, Miller played a much bigger role than he had the previous season. His playing time increased from a total of 24 minutes to 140. He took 22 shots after shooting only five times as a freshman. But his real value was in practice.

"He was there every day," Davis said. "He tried his hardest. You had to have him. We just didn't have enough numbers because basically we had 10 guys. There's a multitude of problems with 10 guys. If anybody gets hurt, then you can't practice five on five. If you only have 10, every guy's in every rep, every drill almost. There's no break.

"He was one guy you didn't have to worry about academically. You didn't have to worry about him in any aspect. He was going to be there every day and give you his best every day. And he actually played in a few games when the game was on the line."

When the season began, Miller was optimistic that the Bearcats could compete in the Big East. After all, that's how it had been during his freshman year. But this team didn't have the talent or the experience that Kennedy's team had. Of those two shortcomings, the lack of experience might have been more crucial than the relative lack of talent.

Maybe Miller should have known from the start that it would be a trying season in the Big East, having been around the league the year before and seeing first-hand how competitive it was.

"We didn't have the players," he said. "Look at the Big East, at least how it used to be. That was brutal, having to go through all those teams. Having to go play at Notre Dame, at Syracuse, at Louisville, it's a bear. But as a player, it's really one game at a time, if there's anything I can do to help, anything I can do to get some playing time. You're in the moment more so than looking and seeing how things are going to play out in the Big East.

"You would go in there just hoping you wouldn't disappoint your coach. They did such a good job of getting your focus on what needs to be happening right now. It was like, yeah, it sucks that we're losing, but here's what we need to be focusing on right now. We've got to be focusing on our next opponent. You could tell he was trying different things. There would be times when he was real hard on us and there were times when he would try to go a little easier and see if we responded better. They were pulling out all the stops."

Miller still had two years of eligibility remaining after the 2006-07 season and saw the program slowly begin to turn into what it is today.

Walk-ons normally don't get much playing time but Branden Miller, pictured here against Notre Dame, saw plenty of action, even against the better teams in the rugged Big East.

He was a model walk-on, a local kid grateful to be playing for the team he grew up following. He was also a good student, which helped to boost the team grade point average in a program desperate to avoid additional academic sanctions. And because Cronin was so short-handed, he was allotted more playing time than most walk-ons.

"Growing up as a Bearcat fan, it was a dream come true," he said. "I think I would have rather won and sat the bench more, but I'm just happy I was able to come in and help them any way I was able to. I was happy to be a part of it, blessed to be a part of this program. You tell people that I had the pleasure to walk on at the University of Cincinnati, that's big time. When they come out with the greatest college programs of all time, UC is always up there. You see the teams that have been to the tournament for how many straight years and UC is always up there. This is a great place to be. I'm a proud alum.

"I still feel like we're a part of the program, like we helped to rebuild it, like we had to try to keep the ship from sinking."

Miller is married and lives in the Cincinnati suburb of Newtown. He graduated in Spring, 2009 with a Bachelor in Business Administration degree in Finance. He works as a wine consultant for Heidelberg Distributing.

Chapter 9

'THAT'S THE STYLE I LIKE TO PLAY'

After they absorbed the beating from Ohio State, the Bearcats had a full week to regroup for North Carolina State. The Wolfpack were in their first year under head coach Sydney Lowe, who played on the 1983 NC State national championship team that defeated Houston's Phi Slamma Jamma team in one of the greatest upsets in NCAA Tournament history. Lowe had replaced former Miami (Ohio) head coach Herb Sendek after Sendek left for Arizona State. Like Cronin, Lowe was in the early stages of a rebuilding job and was operating with a thin roster.

Regardless of their opponent, the Bearcats were eager to get back on the court after the way they were manhandled by the Buckeyes.

"Nobody is used to that and nobody is willing to get used to that," Allen said before the game, "so it's very important for the whole program to bounce back and make sure they're ready for North Carolina State. You never want to hold onto a loss like that."

The Wolfpack played without starting point guard Engin Astur, who was sidelined for the sixth straight game with a hamstring injury. The Bearcats took full advantage of Astur's absence to force 32 turnovers, just three off the school record of 35 that Cleveland State committed against the 1971-72 Bearcats.

It helped that the Wolfpack played with only six scholarship players, giving Cronin the chance to coach against a team with even more severe roster limitations than the Bearcats.

"We trapped them every time they threw a pass," Cronin said. "We just ran out and trapped them everywhere. They actually had a guy throw a pass to a guy who wasn't looking. It hit him in the chest, we grabbed it and laid it in. I've never seen anything like it."

The Bearcats trailed by seven points in the first half, but led by three at halftime. They outscored NC State, 50-38, in the second half as they repeatedly turned turnovers into transition baskets, and won 80-71.

"That's more like the style of play that I like to play," Cronin said after the game. "That's very similar to the way I liked to play at Murray State. We finally found a team that we were deeper than so we could employ the style that you're hopefully going to see from Cincinnati basketball in the future."

Vaughn recovered from his poor outing against Ohio State to score 25 points. He made 10 of 19 shots from the field and recorded nine assists with six steals.

The Bearcats followed with a 60-52 victory over Miami (Ohio) at U.S. Bank Arena in downtown Cincinnati, rallying late after the RedHawks wiped out a three-point deficit to take a 52-50 lead with 4:12 to play.

Vaughn scored only six points, but Sikes had a double-double of 15 points and 10 rebounds. Gentry, who had missed nine straight shots over his last three games, scored eight points on 4-of-7 shooting.

Warren came up big for the Bearcats with 15 points and only one turnover in 32 minutes while making six of nine from the field. Two of his baskets came in the final 2:14 with the game on the line.

——— JAMUAL WARREN ———
Guard, Springfield, Massachusetts

'The hardest thing I have ever done in my life'

During one of the Bearcats' early pre-season practices, Warren delivered what he thought was a nifty one-handed pass that resulted in a dunk for Sikes. Cronin abruptly stopped practice.

"I was like, what the hell?" Warren said. "And then he broke down my whole life with just that one pass. He said, 'Yeah, the pass got through, but that's just like your whole life. You just do enough to get by. You don't want to put two hands on the ball.' Up to that point in my life, that's what I used to do. When stuff got hard, I would do just enough to get by. Just with little stuff like that, that's what changed me as a person. I never really got coached before. Mick was the first person that actually coached me."

Warren grew up in Springfield, Massachusetts, with three brothers and a sister who were raised by a single mother. His mom worked two jobs, which left Warren with plenty of time to get into trouble.

"I was able to do whatever I wanted," Warren said. "I knew my father, but he really didn't come around a lot. I was just a wild, little knuckleheaded kid selling drugs, making excuses, fighting, running with the wrong crowd, with my head in the wrong place with nowhere to turn. I always said to myself as a kid that either I'm going to the Army or I'm going to be able to go to college. It just so happened that I could play basketball, and I started pursuing that. That's what started changing me."

Warren said he was arrested twice and spent 30 days in a boot camp. He played at six different schools, including three junior colleges, before Cronin signed him to play at Cincinnati. He calls UC his savior.

During his playing days he loved to talk to reporters, who sought him out because of the colorful quotes he provided. But there were times when he was a little too talkative to suit Cronin, who would declare Warren temporarily off-limits for interviews.

"I did like talking to reporters," Warren said, "especially about stuff that I feel. If you ask me how I feel about stuff, I'm going to tell you. He used to tell me all the time, you're not talking today."

The 6-foot-2, 195-pound point guard turned 23 during his first year with the Bearcats. He was hard-nosed and a deft passer, just the kind of player Cronin was looking for to run his offense. But he was not a great shooter.

"His passing was a lot better than he got credit for," Cronin said. "A lot of his passes went to 6-5 and 6-6 guys that couldn't finish over Roy Hibbert or Hasheem Thabeet or Aaron Gray."

Warren's last school before Cincinnati was the Globe Institute of Technology, a private, for-profit school in Manhattan which is no longer in operation. He averaged 22.2 points, 4.6 rebounds, 5.9 assists and 3.7 steals and became a second-team juco All-American.

"I went over and watched him in an all-star game," Davis said, "and there was no question he was one of the best available guys. He was borderline talented enough to play at this level. He couldn't really shoot, but he could do everything else and he was tough as nails. The kid had his issues off the court, never anything major, always fringe, but he was a good soul in terms of he was down to win, he was down to fight. He was down to do whatever he needed to do to win. He had a tough life, but you had to take a few flyers on guys and manage them."

Warren started 26 of Cincinnati's 30 games. He averaged 8.0 points and 3.2 assists in 29.2 minutes per game. His best game was against West Virginia, when he scored 16 points with five assists and only one turnover in 41 minutes in the Bearcats' overtime victory.

When Cronin offered him a scholarship, Warren didn't hesitate to accept it.

"I played in a junior college all-star game and I did well and Cronin came up to me and said, 'Hey, do you want to come to Cincinnati?' " Warren remembered. "I said, 'Hell yeah,' He said, 'Do you want to come on a visit?' And I was like, no, I don't need a visit. I don't want a visit. That's where I've been wanting to go.

"I'm from a rough neighborhood. I'd watch them play (on TV), I'd look at the bench and I'd be like, these guys play like how I want go play. So when he came up to me and I saw the C-paw and he said, 'My name is Mick Cronin. I'm the new head coach at Cincinnati, how would you like to come here?' I said, 'Hell, yeah,' just like that. I had to pass four classes in the summertime living in New York City just to go to Cincinnati. That was something people didn't think I was going to do, but I did it.

"Once I got there, I was thinking I did everything else. I went to three junior colleges," Warren said. "I was like, how much harder could it be?"

Warren had always wanted to play for Huggins. But even with Huggins gone, he was still eager for the chance to play for the Bearcats. Having been through so much in his life, having attended so many schools to reach that point, he thought he was prepared for whatever Cronin would throw at him.

He was wrong.

"I tell everybody this: that it is the hardest thing that I have ever done in my life," Warren said. "I felt like when I got there that I had made it. But before we started playing games, that was the hardest time in my life. I called home seven times talking about how I was ready to come home.

"Everywhere else I went, I was the best player all the time. At the other schools the coaches might yell at me, but Mick, he used to just tear me up all the time. To this day, that Bearcat mentality, I take that to work with me. I've been working (at my current job) for a year and I've already jumped two spots. What he wanted out of us was the part that you don't know you have. He pulled that out of you.

"At first I was like, man, what is this dude talking about? But then after awhile as I was going through it, I realized everything he was trying to do to us. Everything I do, I still think about him. If there's a decision to be made, I think about what would Coach do? How would

Jamual Warren learned a lot about basketball from Cronin, but what really matters to him is what he learned about how to lead a good life.

he feel about it? He made me realize who I am and what I could be in my life. He taught me so much.

"But it was more than just Mick. It was Coach Davis, too. They were like the perfect combination. When Mick's mad, Larry's not. When Larry's mad, Mick's not. (Cronin) always said it's about principles. You live off your principles. That how I am now. Everything is about principle. It's just being accountable, being a man. You live your life the right way. That's how he wanted us to play, the right way."

Most coaches get into the profession at least partially because they want to have that kind of impact on their players. In college, that motivation sometimes gets lost amid the pressure to win and the exorbitant amount of money that coaches make.

Cronin isn't immune from either of those factors, and this isn't to suggest that every relationship he has with a player is perfect. But as the son of a high school coach, perhaps he has held onto that original motivation longer than most.

Of Warren, Cronin said: "He's very bright. He just had grown up tough. Some guys struggle when they can't do the work. Other guys just haven't had the proper upbringing, but they've got all the mental capacity in the world. It all goes back to he had to learn to do what he's told or he's never going to be able to hold a job and it's going to be everybody else's fault. He gets it now. That's my whole message with these guys. Until you change, you think it's about a one-handed pass, but it's not."

One of Warren's most trying times during his first year at Cincinnati was near the end of the season, when he didn't start for two straight games after starting the previous 21. In a story I wrote about him for the Enquirer on February 25, Warren seemed puzzled and frustrated.

"I don't know what's going on with my situation here," Warren said. "I guess I'm not good enough or whatever, but I'm still trying. I feel like everything I do is wrong, no matter what I do, no matter if I try to talk to somebody, no matter what. I feel like because we're not winning, everything I'm doing is wrong."

At the time, Warren was two for his last 23 from long range, eight for 58 for the season.

"I know I haven't been playing good," Warren said. "I know that. I try to be a good person off the court. I try to do everything they want me to do, but it's like it's never going to work. That's the only frustrating part. What am I supposed to do?"

He returned to start against Seton Hall on February 28 and scored 13 points in the Bearcats' overtime victory. He played in all 45 minutes and committed only one turnover.

But as bad as things got, Warren hung in there, determined to see the process through. He knew it was his last chance.

"I didn't want to move back to Springfield and just be nobody," he said. "One day I got in trouble, probably for being late, and (Cronin) knew that the one thing I didn't want to do was go back to Springfield and be the guy that I used to be. He bought me a one-way bus ticket back to Springfield. He set it right there in my locker and he was like, Jamual, you want to do this and that, here's your ticket. Those are the little things I needed to make me motivated to be a better person. We used to butt heads a lot. That's because we were both aggressive. We're really alike. I believe in hard work and some of his core values."

Warren's two years at Cincinnati were not without incident. Before his senior season he was cited in a November 4 car accident in which he injured his hand. He was cited for driving without a license, driving on the wrong side of the road and leaving the scene of an accident.

"I got suspended for six games," Warren said. "Man, I can still hear him yelling at me right now. The first time I actually saw him (after the accident) he was like, are you OK? Did you call your mom? Do you need anything? That's when he started on me. He was upset at me. That changed my life too. I could have been done right then and there because he could have let me go. That could have been the end for me."

Warren didn't get to play on a winning team during his two years at Cincinnati. He wasn't a star, and he didn't earn a degree. But he says the experience made him a better person and gave him the chance to fulfill one of his life goals.

"I knew I was good," he said, "but I'm a realist. I'm not afraid to admit things that I know. I knew that maybe I wasn't going to go to the NBA. That was never my dream. My dream was that I wanted to be the starting point guard. I wanted to come down the court, stand at the top of the key and call a play. That's all I wanted to do. People said you couldn't go to college. You're not made for college. You'll never go Division I. You'll never be on TV. That was my dream. I didn't care what happened, I was going to do it, no matter how long

it took me. I wanted my mom to say, yeah, this is what he did.

"That's why I never quit. I'm proud of what I did for me and my family. I'm proud that I don't have a police record. That's what matters to me, just living a good life. That's what Cincinnati did for me.

"I remember the older guys (former Cincinnati players) telling me, 'You're like an old-school Bearcat.' And I took that to heart. When I watch them play now, I get mad and upset (when they don't play well) because I know the pain we put in. I feel like they took it and built on it. That's how the foundation was. We might not score a lot, but you might not score a lot either. Now we've got scorers. Now we've got the talent and the hungriness and the readiness, everything that Mick Cronin brings."

After Cincinnati, Warren played one year for CT Top Ballaz in the American Basketball Association. He lives in Pittsfield, Massachusetts, about an hour northwest of Springfield, and works as a printer. He has three kids, one of whom lives in Cincinnati.

"I've got two cars, I own my own house, I have custody of my kids and I'm about to get married," Warren said. "For me, where I grew up and what I was coming from, it's like night and day. I come to Cincinnati once every three months to see my son. I call J-Will, Deonta. Those are my friends for life for the stuff we went through. We went 2-14 in the Big East but we stuck together and built a bond that has never been broken."

CHAPTER 10

MEMPHIS BLUES

After the Bearcats beat North Carolina State and Miami, they were 9-3, having also beaten Xavier and Temple. It was a better-than-expected start for a team that just a few months earlier had been scouring the country for players.

There was a feeling among some fans that maybe the season wouldn't be so bad after all. Even Cronin briefly fell into the trap of optimism.

"In my mind I'm thinking maybe I'll be able to skirt through this and then we'll be better next year because they're all back and we've got freshmen coming in," Cronin said. "But then reality sunk in. You just couldn't trick anybody anymore. If you're tricking people in November and December, people figure out how you're tricking them, how you're hiding all of your weaknesses and deficiencies. You can't hide it in conference play."

The Bearcats didn't have to wait for conference play to have the wheels fall off what was a shakily constructed vehicle to start with. It started with a 79-66 loss to Ohio U. on December 30 at Quicken Loans Arena in Cleveland. This wasn't Ohio State they were losing to. It was OU, not a bad program but certainly not a powerhouse. The Bobcats went 19-13 overall, 9-7 in the Mid-American Conference that season.

The game was won on the free throw line, where OU made 30 of 36 foul shots compared with 12 of 15 for the Bearcats. Coaches normally blame officials for such a wide disparity in free throws, but Cronin said his players had no one to blame but themselves.

"That was our worst defensive effort of the season," Cronin said after the game. "We got exactly what we deserved. No matter what we tried to do it was a feeble attempt. The enormous amount of free throws that they attempted was a direct result of our poor defense."

The Bearcats also committed 18 turnovers against OU's half-court zone defense and a rather passive 1-2-2 zone press.

"We just threw the ball away for no reason," Cronin.

After trailing 37-26 at halftime, the Bearcats scored the first six points of the second half and appeared on the verge of a comeback. But they played from eight to 10 points behind for most of the second half. Cincinnati made 26 field goals to 22 for the Bobcats, but couldn't stop its incessant fouling.

While I was in the media room settling in to write my game story, Cronin called my cell phone.

"You've got to do me a favor," he said.

Cronin asked me to write something about why he missed his post-game radio show. The radio crew was not stationed on the floor as it is in most college arenas. Cronin didn't know where he was supposed to go, and no one showed him. Yes, he was upset by the loss, he said, but he had every intention of doing his post-game radio interview. I wrote his explanation in my post-game notes package, not as a favor, but because I felt fans would want to know why there was no post-game interview.

The Bearcats had one more game to play before beginning Big East play. That was against Memphis, a long-time rival in Conference USA.

When Cincinnati was invited to join the Big East along with Louisville, South Florida, DePaul and Marquette from C-USA, Memphis and UAB were left out. The Bearcats agreed to play both schools in a home-and-home series as part of an agreement that allowed Cincinnati to keep the NCAA Tournament shares it had accrued as a member of C-USA.

The 23rd-ranked Tigers, then coached by John Calipari, had a decided advantage in talent. They also had lots of motivation considering that Memphis had lost eight of its last 10 games against the Bearcats, although the Tigers had won the most recent meeting between the two rivals 91-81 on December 3, 2005 at Fifth Third Arena.

Cronin had warned his players that many of their opponents would view this season as a chance to get even for all the times Cincinnati had beaten up on them in recent years. Already the Bearcats had lost to UAB and Ohio. Now they were preparing to go on the road to face a ranked Memphis team that was no doubt looking forward to playing them.

"I've watched Cincinnati beat a lot of teams," Warren said before the game, "especially Memphis. They've been going at it and Memphis does not like Cincinnati. I know that for a fact. They think we're soft right now and they're going to sneak a couple of wins, but we ain't laying down. I know that."

"It'll be interesting," Cronin said, "because Cincinnati has not always been the favorite team to Memphis fans. That's Coach Huggins' fault. He won a lot of games down there. I told the guys nobody thinks we can win but us."

With 10 players averaging 10 minutes per game and no player logging more than 28 minutes per game, Memphis was the direct opposite of Cincinnati. Plus, the Tigers were 8-0 at home.

On the afternoon of the game, I made the drive down to Oxford, Mississippi, to interview Kennedy for a story about his new job at Ole Miss and drove back the 85 miles to Memphis in a driving rain. The game against the Tigers was played in FedEx Forum, home of the NBA Memphis Grizzlies. Cronin was right. The Memphis fans were lying in wait for the struggling Bearcats.

There was one fan in particular I remembered from the Huggins era. He sat about 10 rows behind the media, on the same side as the Cincinnati bench. He was always well-dressed and knew how to make himself heard. He would have plenty to crow about on this night.

The game was being televised nationally on ESPN2 – at least the first half was. The Bearcats fell behind 11-0 and trailed by 31 points at halftime. As the 88-55 blowout unfolded, I watched Cronin periodically pause and look futilely at his bench for someone who could stop this massacre.

Then I heard the guy who used to ride Huggins. "Hey, Mick! Mick!" he yelled. "This never happened when Huggins was the coach!"

But it was happening now and it was all too real. There was nothing Cronin could do except stand there and take it and not react to the jeering fan. The score was so lopsided at halftime that ESPN2 switched to the USC-Oregon game.

The Cincinnati-Memphis game started at 9 p.m. Eastern time, which meant I was on a tight deadline back in the day when newspapers actually cared about getting late results in the

Warren proved his doubters wrong when he became the starting point guard at Cincinnati.

next day's edition. Before the game, I mentioned to the Cincinnati media contact, that if it were possible I needed to talk to Cronin for a few seconds before he did his post-game radio show so I could get a few quotes in my story.

But when Cronin emerged from the Cincinnati locker room, he was in no mood to talk to me. The sports information contact tried to intercede. "Coach, can you talk to Bill real quick? He's on a tight deadline."

Cronin kept walking. "I'll talk to him after I do my radio show," he snapped.

Then he stopped and turned around. "Do you really need to talk to me now?" he asked.

I told him that I did, if only for a minute or two. Then he waited for me to ask a question. In more than 20 years of covering college basketball I had never been speechless after a game. I might not have always asked an intelligent question, but I always had something to ask.

Not this time.

"I don't know what to ask," I said, like a kid just out of college covering his first game.

Most coaches would have turned and walked away, but Cronin began to talk about the game, although it was obvious that he, too, didn't really know what to say.

"I thought we played pretty well the first 10 minutes or so," he said. "We got good shots. We were moving the ball. They just made every shot. There was nothing we could do. If they shot the ball like that, we weren't going to win. The worst nightmare happened."

I've always remembered that as the low point in Cronin's rebuilding process, although others have pointed to the Bearcats' 96-51 drubbing at the hands of Connecticut during his second year. I've told the story about my post-game failure to ask a question after the Memphis game many times, and Cronin and I have laughed about it. But it wasn't funny at the time for either of us.

"We had to be able to keep the game at a certain pace where teams couldn't score quickly because we didn't have enough firepower," Cronin said. "When a team like Memphis made all those shots, we couldn't do that. And we ran into a coach who understood if you don't let Vaughn shoot and don't let Marvin (Gentry) shoot, they can't score inside. So if Sikes couldn't pop out and make shots on their center, we had no answer.

"People started figuring out when we run all those screens for Vaughn, just switch. Xavier didn't, so we were able to get Deonta free in that game. Calipari and the Big East schools after that, they figured out that when they run that stuff for Vaughn, just switch so we couldn't get him open. He was a guy that needed screens. He was like a Steve Alford. He couldn't get his own shot. If a team figured us out, we couldn't just say, 'OK, we're going to man up and play you.' We needed strategy to score."

Vaughn took only seven shots and scored eight points against the Tigers. McGowan scored 20 points on seven-of-nine shooting. The only other Bearcat to reach double figures was Williamson with 11 points, but he needed 14 shots to get them. Cincinnati was out-rebounded 42-23.

"That was a rough one," Sikes said.

That left the Bearcats with a 9-5 record as they headed into Big East play. By then, they knew what awaited them, but they refused to concede anything.

"There was no game we went into where we were like, oh, we're about to lose," Warren said.

Cincinnati's first Big East game was at home against Rutgers, traditionally one of the conference also-rans, so there was every reason to believe they could start league play on a positive note regardless of what had happened against Memphis and Ohio U. The Scarlet Knights, in their first season under head coach Fred Hill, were 7-7, were averaging only 62.4 points, and shooting 41.3 percent from the field. They had already lost their Big East opener, 77-72 to Seton Hall.

The Bearcats had two primary concerns as they prepared for Rutgers. They had to improve on defense and they had to find a way to get Vaughn more involved in the offense. In their losses to Memphis and Ohio, the Bearcats allowed an average of 83.5 points. In their nine wins they had allowed 57.9 points per game. In their first five losses, they had surrendered 77.8.

"Our defense is not where it needs to be," Cronin said before the game. "Needless to say, we need to keep people around 55 or 57, like we did against Xavier, to have a chance against good teams."

Vaughn, who averaged 16.9 points in his first nine games, was held to 9.5 in his next five, as opponents began to focus on stopping him.

"We need to get him more shots," Cronin said.

That didn't happen against Rutgers. In one of their worst offensive performances of the season, the Bearcats were shut down in a 54-42 loss to the Scarlet Knights before 8,212 fans at Fifth Third Arena. Vaughn continued to struggle, with just two points on one-of-10 shooting. Cincinnati attempted only six free throws.

Cronin was so upset that he met with his players for an hour and 15 minutes after the game. It took nearly two hours before they emerged from their locker room to speak with reporters.

"It's going to be his way, or people aren't going to be part of this team," Warren said. "He wants to win and he wants us to get better. We're not playing Bearcat basketball or whatever people want to call it."

Cincinnati had been outscored 33-22 in the second half, which raised the question: If the Bearcats couldn't win at home against Rutgers, supposedly one of the worst teams in the league, what could Cronin tell Cincinnati fans to make them believe things would get any better before the season ended in March?

Cronin didn't have the answer.

"That's the million-dollar question," he said.

Then he unloaded.

"Our effort is going to get better," he said. "I'm not happy right now and the guys know it. I haven't talked about winning and losing all year because of my concern with our lack of depth and lack of personnel as we head into the Big East.

"Effort is what matters. Playing hard is what matters. Being good guys is what matters. Never quitting and playing with courage is what matters. That's what we've preached all year, that the results take care of themselves if you take care of those things. We've been squeezing blood from a rock. We need a couple days off to try to refresh because we're a team that right now is very fragile."

Ron Allen played only three minutes against Rutgers, after being held out of the Memphis game altogether because Cronin said he hadn't been practicing hard enough. Allen didn't play in the following game against South Florida, and after logging six minutes against Syracuse on January 17, he didn't play again until January 31 at Louisville, when he got on the floor for two minutes. That wasn't what Allen had in mind when the season began, given that he was one of only two scholarship players returning from the previous season.

——— RON ALLEN ———
Forward, Los Angeles, California

'We didn't have a chance'

As soon as he heard that Kennedy wouldn't return, Allen began to worry. He felt he had come a long way during his junior year under Kennedy and was poised to make a larger contribution his senior year. But now with Kennedy leaving, he would have a new head coach with a new system. More importantly, he would have to earn the head coach's trust all over again.

"I felt like I was going to have a really strong, solid senior year," Allen said. "When they said that they didn't bring him back, I didn't know what to expect. It put me back into limbo as a basketball player. I didn't know if I would be kept or if they would clean house. I didn't know any of those things."

Allen's journey to Cincinnati began with Hurricane Katrina in August, 2005, while he was playing at Xavier, an NAIA school in New Orleans. When the levees broke, the school was evacuated and Allen headed for Shreveport, Louisiana, where he stayed with the family of a friend.

As improbable as it seemed at the time, a week later he was in Cincinnati, as a member of the Bearcats' basketball team, preparing to play in the Big East.

"Fortunately we got out before the levees broke," Allen said. "We didn't experience any flooding because we evacuated."

When his former AAU coach, Rick Isaacs, called to see if he was OK, Allen told him he would be willing to relocate to another city if he could continue his college basketball career. The previous year at Xavier he had played in 19 games, averaging 4.9 points and 2.6 rebounds. He was sure he could do better and was eager to get a chance on a bigger stage.

About 90 minutes later, Isaacs called him back with Kennedy on the line.

"My AAU coach sold me to Andy as far as my athleticism and energy and positivity and my size and what I could bring to the table," Allen said. "Coach Huggs had been relieved of his duties and it allowed for a scholarship to open up. Ivan Johnson decided that he didn't want to come because Huggs wouldn't be coaching. So there was a scholarship open and there was also a position at the forward position that would have been tailor-made for a player like me.

"Andy Kennedy right then and there on the phone said, 'If you can get here in four or five days we'll offer you a full athletic scholarship,' based on what my guy had told him. He had never seen me play."

After Allen arrived in Cincinnati and worked out for Kennedy,

Andy called to tip me off. "This will be a national story," he said excitedly.

It never became a national story to my knowledge, but it was still a good story – a refugee from Hurricane Katrina arrives in Cincinnati to help fortify a Bearcat basketball program that had been decimated by Huggins' firing.

It would have been a much better story if Allen had been a more productive player, which Kennedy assured me he would be.

Allen was – and still is - one of the most self-assured people I've ever encountered. But Kennedy oversold him as a player. He didn't fit what Cronin was looking for in the early stages of his rebuilding process. He was a 6-foot-9, 235-pound forward who preferred to shoot from the perimeter in a program that was emphasizing physical toughness, defense and rebounding.

Allen made it a point to attend Cronin's introductory press conference because he wanted to be the first Cincinnati player the new coach saw.

"It was awkward because I could tell that he already had his mind made up that he wasn't going to have an emphasis on me," Allen said. "I felt the energy that I wasn't going to get a fair (chance) because of him being a young coach and seeing things the way he wanted to see things coming in. I think it kind of impressed him that I came to the press conference, and when we shook hands I may have re-set his opinion about me. Our player-coach relationship was night and day compared with our man-to-man relationship. I'm not the type of player that he liked and vice-versa. He kept me because I was a senior and he's a good guy."

Allen now blames himself for his lack of playing time, saying that he was too immature to help his own cause.

"We never really got on the same page," Allen said. "He had a lot of things that he was still trying to figure out as a young coach at that level, and me not being fully mature at that time and not understanding how to make his job easier as a player, as a senior leader, it was very, very inconsistent, up and down, hit and miss. There were just so many instances where it was so easy for us to be on the same page and yet we weren't.

"He wanted me to rebound," Allen said. "He wanted me to do all the dirty stuff, and I didn't want to do that. I wanted to be a star. I wanted to score. I wanted things to be built around me. I wanted to put up a resume where I could help my team win, get to the tournament and get drafted. Our agendas didn't match up, and him being the head coach, he didn't play me."

Under Kennedy, Allen had played in 33 games with three starts and averaged 7.3 minutes per game. Under Cronin, he played in 20 games with one start. He averaged 2.4 points and 1.6 rebounds under Kennedy, making 11-for-27 from three-point range and shooting 41.3 percent from the field. As a senior he made two of 12 three-pointers, shot 32.3 percent from the field and averaged 1.3 points and 1.1 rebounds.

"He's a great kid," Davis said. "He just wasn't quite good enough to help us. He thought he was a jump shooter and the last thing we needed was a jump-shooting 6-9 guy who wasn't that good of a

Ron Allen realizes now that he should have been more willing to do the dirty work that might have earned him more playing time.

shooter."

As one of only two seniors on the team, Allen attempted to be a leader. But his attempts to fill that role weren't well-received because he didn't play enough for his words to carry much weight.

"Nobody wanted to hear Ronald Allen tell everybody what they needed to do to prepare for Louisville and Seton Hall and Notre Dame," Allen said. "We had some matchups where I knew the way we were winning games early wasn't going to be good enough. Mick knew, but you also have to have an advocate on the team as a player, and McGowan didn't want any part of any leadership. Mick came in and made Ced a captain, and the team didn't respond to that because they knew Ced's not a leader, so I'm doing Ced's job. Mick didn't want that because that puts pressure on him to play me. That put him in a bind."

Allen can see how difficult the situation was, not only for the players but also for the coaches.

"Coach Huggs had it going there," he said. "Then to go from that to the third head coach in three years, to guys who honestly never would have been Cincinnati-type players except for the sense of urgency to get guys, and now they're trying to figure out what they need to do at that level to be successful. It was shaky on all fronts. We didn't have a guy on the team mature enough to rally us and get us focused. We didn't have a roster that was mature enough, and I'm including myself."

Allen is the only player I interviewed who said the players didn't get along.

"Guys didn't like each other," he said, "just trying to keep that together, keep that from blowing up, and then you've got coaches who didn't really care about that dynamic. They were just trying to keep their job. And then you've got Mick as a young coach trying to manage all that at the same time. Lord knows what he was going through from an administrative standpoint. We didn't have a chance."

The Ohio State game was especially frustrating for Allen, who played only six minutes, "especially watching Greg Oden do what he was doing and knowing what I could do to him if I was allowed to play."

Allen took two shots against the Buckeyes, both three-pointers, and missed them. He had no rebounds and two fouls to show for his brief time on the floor.

"I take the onus on myself," Allen said. "I didn't want to do what was needed for me to help the team get better. As a coach now, I understand that if you're asking a player to defend and rebound and he doesn't want to do that, you don't get minutes. But I wasn't mature at the time. Me and Mick didn't have a relationship where we could sit down and he could explain it to me. And he's a young coach and he's just trying to manage the situation. He don't have time for the senior to keep asking what do I need to do to get minutes."

Before his final game with the Bearcats, Allen proclaimed in an interview that he would play in the NBA someday. I asked him if he was sure he wanted to say that because it would make him look foolish, given that he didn't play that much at Cincinnati. But he didn't back down. If anything, he doubled down. He really believed it. The headline of the story I wrote in the Enquirer read, "Allen's NBA dream hasn't been idled."

"I know I can play in the NBA," he said in that February 27 story. "It's just a matter of getting the blessing to do so and me getting the opportunity. Nothing will break my confidence. Basketball has been my dream since I was a little kid. The only thing that will stop me from playing basketball is injury. I'm going to play basketball until I can't play anymore because of my love for it. I know what I'm capable of. The things that I'm good at, I feel I can get paid for.

"I'm a very athletic power forward or small forward and I can shoot the ball. With the right coaching and the right guidance I feel like I can be a really good player."

Allen came closer to the NBA than anyone who heard him talk that day would have predicted. He played for four years in the NBA's Development League, averaging 5.9 points and 3.1 rebounds in 16.5 minutes per game for five different teams before a back injury ended his career. "I went to training camp with the Maine Red Claws, but my back just wasn't right," Allen said. "I felt that the entire training camp. I knew I was done. The last day of training camp I told the coaching staff that I was going to retire at 28 years old. That was one of the toughest days of my life."

For the past few years, Allen has worked as a development coach/trainer. He has also worked as an assistant coach at LA Pierce College.

"I also own a clothing business called Committed to Greatness," he said. "We sell T-shirts, sweat suits, hoodies, hats. I'm taking care of my family, coaching basketball. I'm healthy, I'm happy. I have a very strong, growing relationship with Coach Cronin and other people in my network. Walter Lewis, who was a walk-on on that team, is one of my best friends. I'm married, I have an 8-year-old son and a 6-year-old daughter.

"I take from that year that I should have done more of what I can control. I should have rebounded better. I should have defended better. I shouldn't have been so selfish thinking only about me. I should have been more in tune with what's best for the team and what I can do to get us there. I thank Coach Cronin for keeping a relationship with me because he's one of my guys now. We've both grown and learned a lot. I'm so proud of him and where has that program right now."

Allen graduated in Spring, 2007, with a Bachelor of Science degree in Criminal Justice and was recently hired as the head coach at Inglewood High School in Los Angeles, his hometown.

And yes, he still believes he'll end up in the NBA someday.

"I tell everybody that I didn't make it as a player, but I'll make it as a coach," Allen said. "I'm going to make it in the NBA because I know I'm waking up every day and I'm pursuing this dream."

Chapter 11

TEARS OF FRUSTRATION

After their loss to Memphis, the Bearcats had a full week to practice before their first Big East road game, at South Florida. As had been the case with Rutgers, they were facing one of the conference's lesser lights. And in this case, they were facing a team they had regularly beaten up on in C-USA, although the Bulls had beaten the Bearcats the year before.

When they took the floor at the Sun Dome in Tampa, they were trying to avoid Cincinnati's first four-game losing streak since the 1987-88 season, Tony Yates' second-to-last as head coach. In addition, the Bearcats hadn't started a conference season with two straight losses since January 1987, when they lost to Metro Conference foes Southern Miss and Memphis State.

USF was 0-3 in the Big East and had lost 18 of its 19 conference games since joining the league the previous year. But like almost every Big East team the Bearcats faced, USF had at least one big, strong physical player that they couldn't match up with. For the Bulls, that player was Kentrell Gransberry, a 6-foot-9, 270-pound monster of a transfer from LSU who was averaging 14.1 points and 10.3 rebounds while shooting 62.8 percent from the floor.

The Bearcats trailed at halftime 35-24, then were outscored 17-3 at the start of the second half falling behind by 25. Trailing 52-27 with

11:44 left, they scored 16 straight points to get within nine with 9:21 left, but the comeback fizzled after that and they fell 74-59.

Cincinnati shot 33.3 percent from the field and made just seven of 30 three-pointers. UC was out-rebounded 41-37 and its front line was outscored 54-10. The Bearcats committed 28 fouls that resulted in 35 USF free throws, 22 of which the Bulls converted.

Gransberry scored 21 points and pulled down 15 rebounds against Cincinnati's unimposing front line.

Vaughn scored 21 points to lead the Bearcats, but he made only seven of his 22 shots. Cincinnati's starting front line of Sikes, McGowan and Williamson managed only 10 points among them on four-of-18 shooting.

As I talked to Cronin outside the Bearcats' locker room after the game, he told me that McGowan had been in the locker room crying. Oddly enough, he viewed that as a positive.

"That's the first time this year after a loss that we've had a guy get really emotional," he said. "In real programs, with teams that achieve things, losses rip your heart out."

Since he arrived in Cincinnati, Cronin has never allowed reporters into his locker room after games, except during the conference tournament and the NCAA Tournament, which mandate that locker rooms be opened to the media 10 minutes after a game ends. Huggins and Yates had the same policy.

By the time Cronin mentioned McGowan's tears, the senior forward was already on the bus. I went outside and asked if he would get off to talk to me, which he did.

"It's getting old now," McGowan said, still fighting back tears an hour after the game. "We've lost four in a row. We just need to come together as a team so we can win. We're not supposed to be happy after we lose. One of the reasons I'm so emotional right now is that I'm worried that they're going to get used to losing and quit and just turn it in. I don't want that to happen in my senior year."

McGowan's tears also made an impact on Warren.

"This is his last chance," Warren said. "I know how it feels to have a last chance. I feel bad because he's a senior and it's almost over for him. He's had two sets of players in two years so he's frustrated and it made me feel upset. We're not going to get used to losing. There's no getting used to it."

——— CEDRIC MCGOWAN ———
Forward, Miami, Florida

'We were going to fight, we were going to claw'

When I first came up with the idea for this book, the player I most wanted to talk to was McGowan. He was also the most difficult to reach, which didn't surprise me. He was the one player from that team with whom all of his teammates had lost contact.

As I thought about how difficult the season must have been for the other players, McGowan stood out at the player who had endured the most. He has signed with the Bearcats while Huggins was still the head coach, only to hear in summer of 2005, when he

Cedric McGowan chose Cincinnati because he admired the Bearcats' take-no-prisoners style of play.

was getting ready to head to Cincinnati, that Huggins had been fired.

McGowan was another of the players on Cronin's first team who was a Cincinnati fan from having watched the Bearcats play on TV. He admired their take-no-prisoners style.

"For me, it was like, I know this sucks, but I wouldn't want to go nowhere else," McGowan said of Huggins' departure. "Cincinnati basketball was what I lived for, just the style of play. I couldn't see myself playing for no other school. It was like, OK, Huggs isn't there, but I still get the opportunity to play in the Big East."

The 6-foot-7, 225-pound McGowan, sporting his trademark dreadlocks, started 33 of 34 games for the 2005-06 Bearcats. He averaged 8.5 points and 7.2 rebounds on a team that went 21-13 and advanced to the quarterfinals of the NIT under Kennedy.

"There really wasn't any pressure on Andy because he had been there a while," McGowan said. "He and (assistant coach) Frank Martin were familiar with how I played and what I could bring. Mick, he really wasn't as familiar with who I was, my role, and what I could do. It was me learning him as much as him learning me. For Mick, it was a lot of pressure, being a first-year coach."

When Kennedy didn't get the job after his interim year, McGowan decided to stay and get his degree, even though the circumstances would be much more difficult. Almost all of his teammates from the previous year would be gone, and he'd be playing on a team that from a pure talent standpoint didn't have a chance to win consistently in the Big East.

McGowan knew all that but figured Cincinnati was still the best place for him to finish his college career.

"I could have easily transferred," he said. "But my whole thing was, why leave? My ultimate goal was to get my degree. I had to make a decision to go somewhere else, sit out a year, get a degree and get better being in a whole different place, or just stay where I'm at, get my degree, and figure things out after that. So I made the decision to just stay and get my degree.

"I love Andy Kennedy and the way he does things. I was actually contemplating when he left to follow him and Frank Martin wherever they went. But did I want to go to another state and sit out a year? It probably would have benefited me, but I figured I'm here at UC where I know all of the professors. I'm getting a degree. I know what I need to do."

Graduating was very important to McGowan, who grew up in

harsh circumstances in inner-city Miami. On the night he shed tears after the loss to USF, he had a large gathering of family members at the game, which made the loss and his four-point performance difficult to handle. He also suffered an injury that night and says that's why he was in tears.

"Most of that was that I was in pain," McGowan said. "I took a charge and hurt my tailbone. That was the first time that all of my family came to support me, the first time ever. We were poor. That was the closest that they could actually get to where everybody could put their money together, get a van, and drive up to see me. They got T-shirts made and everything. It was a good feeling to have my family there to support me.

"My parents were always working. When I was growing up, all the people who supported me were my teammates' parents because they would always be there. Their parents were like my parents. My mom, she had to work. She loved me to death, but money had to be made to take care of the house. Basketball for me was just an outlet to make it out. Because a lot of kids, where I'm from, they didn't make it out. They didn't have goals or anything. For me it was just like tunnel vision.

"I was kind of disappointed that we lost in front of my family and it kind of hit me that maybe we're not as good as we think. We really, really worked hard, but things just wouldn't work out."

Once he understood the full impact of what the Bearcats were facing, McGowan swallowed hard and decided that he would try to make the best of a bad situation.

"We were going to fight, we were going to claw, we were going to bite, we were going to kick, we were going to scratch," McGowan said. "We were going to do whatever we could. If we don't win, then they're just the better team, but we have to make sure we give it our all. That's just the reality of the situation, just to go ahead and do whatever we could to win. If we lost, we just tried to figure out what we didn't do to win and tried to put that together for the next game."

McGowan did his best to instill that attitude in his teammates, but he acknowledges that he wasn't a rah-rah leader. He tried to lead by example.

His teammates understood what he was going through. As bad as it was for them at times, there was also a sense that they were in a good spot, getting to play in the Big East on national television against some of the best teams in the country, something they never expected to do. They weren't there the previous season when Cincinnati was winning. Perhaps they would have appreciated a little more guidance from McGowan, but they also knew he couldn't do something that wasn't in his nature.

"He tried to give us as much advice as he could," Williamson said. "Everybody was frustrated, but Ced was trying to find his way, which is what we were all trying to do. He didn't really show his emotions on being on a team before that should have gone to the NCAA (Tournament). He was just like, we've got to find a way to win. We were leaning on each other. As much as we felt we needed him, I'm sure he felt the same way."

No matter how much McGowan tried not to show it, his

teammates could sense his frustration.

"Me and Ced, we were real good friends," Gentry said. "I know the situation was tough on him. He came from junior college. He transferred here thinking he was going to play for Huggs, then the situation happened with Huggs and he's playing for Andy Kennedy and then the next year he's playing for Mick Cronin. I think he did a good job of not showing any frustration. He was a senior and we looked up to him for leadership. He did anything Coach asked him to and tried to make the best out of the situation."

Said Barwin: "It was hard for him. He had a disappointing year because he was probably our most talented guy. He had a great opportunity and he didn't necessarily take advantage of it. I remember him struggling at times, but he was a hell of a player — a big, physical, talented guy. He just never really got it going."

With so many first-year players, it was difficult for the Bearcats to develop the cohesion that comes with players spending several years together on and off the court, getting acquainted with each other as people as well as teammates. At the same time, the coaching staff was learning about the players they had recruited under a severe time crunch.

"Everybody at that time of year had their own goals," McGowan said. "We were all different. We were all from different parts of the States. On the court we were cool. Off the court we were cool too, but they had their own things going on. It was definitely different compared to James White and Eric Hicks and Jihad Muhammad, Armein Kirkland and all those guys, because they weren't coming into a situation and having to fit in. It was like when Ron came in and then I came in. Everybody else was already there so it was an easier adjustment."

Cronin's style of play and the demands he made also caused McGowan to adjust. McGowan said Cronin's dictates also led to some hesitation on offense.

"In that first year, we had a lot of things that kind of broke my confidence a little bit," McGowan said, "because the shots that we would have to take, we weren't allowed to take because (Cronin) had his rules and the way he wanted to do things. If you're going to take shots, you're going to have some contested shots. But for us, being that it was his first year, if you took a contested shot you were in trouble. We needed to take wide open shots for us to not get into trouble. For me, it was kind of like a confidence breaker.

"Some guys get off from making contested shots. That's what makes the game more competitive. If I can make a shot over you, now I've got you. That's a part of the game. Some guys need that."

McGowan played in all 30 games in 2006-07. He started 24, averaging 8.2 points and scoring in double figures 10 times, with a high of 20 points against Memphis, which tied his career high. His rebounding average slipped from 7.2 to 5.1, but Cronin attributed that to his switch from power forward to small forward, where he was counted on to be more of a passer and perimeter scorer.

Before his last home game against Seton Hall, McGowan said he was proud of what he had accomplished during his two years at Cincinnati.

McGowan's final home game as a Bearcat resulted in a 70-67 overtime victory against Seton Hall.

"The best part has been making something out of nothing," he said. "We came in last year and people didn't expect us to do good and we did better than most people expected. This year people really didn't expect us to do anything, but we did enough to let everybody know that we're trying and that we did our best."

Cronin understood better than anyone how taxing, even awkward, it had to be for him with the change in coaches in addition to playing with two different sets of teammates during his two years.

"He was a power forward at heart," Cronin said. "If he could have gone to a mid-major school and played forward, he'd have been a force. But that highest level, trying to shoot threes, it wasn't his game. It was tough because I was young and crazy and losing was hard on me. He became frustrated because he's a good kid. He wanted to deliver, but he was being played out of position. It just wasn't in him to be a vocal leader. He was the ultimate nice guy, but a quiet guy. So his experience, I feel bad for him. He plays in a year when it was chaos and then he played a year where we're totally outmanned. He never really got to experience any fun at all."

When the season ended, McGowan felt like he was in a daze. His college basketball career was over. He was on schedule to earn a Bachelor of Science degree in Criminal Justice, which he did in Spring, 2007. Now he had to figure out what was next.

"Coming from where I'm from, I was the first person in my family to graduate from high school," he said. "I didn't know what was next. When Chad Johnson came to the Bengals – he's from Miami as well – I had a conversation with him about agents and tried to figure out what's the next step. He gave me some advice, but I didn't know what to do, honestly. I made sure I went by the basketball office every day and said something to somebody. I didn't have any plans to play basketball after that. I went by one day and talked to Mick and he said, 'Hey, these guys are trying to get in contact with you.' Before I knew it, I was going to a senior showcase camp and ended up being the MVP of the camp.

"My first year I played in Finland and averaged 18 and nine. After that, I played in Holland. I didn't have a good year there. I got hurt a lot. I sat out a whole year. After that I went to play in South America for the rest of my career. I played in Colombia, Uruguay, Argentina and Mexico."

McGowan's professional playing career is over. He lives in Jacksonville, Fla., and works as a corrections officer. He has three children.

When he watches the Bearcats and sees the success they've had, he feels a sense of pride in his school, but also a touch of envy. He wishes it could have been him playing in the NCAA Tournament, and he has a hard time believing that he had anything to do with where the program is now because of what he did his senior year.

"I don't feel like I had anything to do with it at the time, that I was there because it was a rebuilding phase," he said. "I only had one year (under Cronin). We made the best out of it whether we did well or we didn't do too well. If anything, all the praise goes to Mick. He's doing a hell of a job turning that program around and doing what he's done from day one and the way he carried himself as a professional on and off the court. My hat's off to him."

Still, McGowan thinks about what his career might have been like if he had been able to play for Huggins.

"I loved Andy Kennedy and how he did things and I loved Mick," McGowan said. "I just think the overall decision to go to Cincinnati with Huggs leaving, I wish I could go back and do that all over again because I feel if Huggs was still there, I would probably still be in the (NBA) right now."

Chapter 12

ORANGE CRUSHER

By January 5, the Bearcats already had two Big East games under their belt after the loss to USF, but you could make a case that they had yet to truly experience quintessential Big East basketball. That was about to change, with a trip to Syracuse to play in the Carrier Dome. The Orange were a founding member of the Big East and one of its premier programs, with Hall of Fame coach Jim Boeheim presiding over his customary 2-3 zone defense.

Boeheim's annoying zone was the last thing the Bearcats wanted to see after shooting 35 percent over their last three games against Memphis, Rutgers and USF. Syracuse was long and disciplined and made it difficult for even talented, experienced teams to locate quality shots, especially around the basket. To beat them you needed accurate outside shooters and patience – lots of patience.

By then Cincinnati's losing streak had grown to four games. Now the Bearcats were trying to avoid the school's first 0-3 conference start since 1983-84, when they went 0-12 in the Metro Conference. Syracuse, led by Demetrius Nichols with 18.9 points per game, was 14-4 overall, 3-1 in the Big East and had held each of its last four opponents under 40 percent shooting.

Complicating matters for the Bearcats, Williamson entered the game mired in a scoring slump. After averaging 15.6 points in his first 11 games, he had averaged only 8.0 in his next five. He attempted only four shots against USF and scored just two points before fouling out. He had made seven of 25 shots in his last three games and was complaining of pain from tendinitis in both knees.

"He's got to get back to being aggressive," Cronin said. "He was stuffing the stat sheet early in the season and he's got to get back to doing that because we don't have anybody else to stuff the stat sheet."

The Bearcats did have a little recent history on their side, though. The year before they knocked off the Orange 82-65 on the road, getting 19 points and nine rebounds from McGowan.

Cincinnati's bid to win at Syracuse a second straight time was led by Sikes, who made eight of 12 three-pointers to fuel a comeback that fell agonizingly short at the end. He had entered the game having made 18 of 44 from long range for the season for 40.9 percent.

Firing away over the zone, Sikes recorded his first trey with 8:12 left in the first half. The next came at the 5:02 mark. He made two more before halftime.

"After I made about three or four of them, I felt like if I throw this one up, this one will go in too," Sikes said after the game.

He picked up where he left off early in the second half and kept firing away. His eight three-point goals in one game still rank as the third-most in school history.

The underdog Bearcats fell behind by 19 in the first half, however, and they trailed by 14 at halftime. But they scored 10 straight points in the second half, starting with a three-pointer from the top of the key by Warren with 7:07 left, and trailed by just one 68-67 with 4:43 left.

A three-pointer by Eric Devendorf gave the Orange a four-point lead, but Sikes hit his seventh three of the game with 3:53 left and his eighth with 1:09 to play to give the Bearcats their first lead of the game at 75-73. When Gentry's free throw made it 76-73 with 43 seconds left, the crowd of 22,248 couldn't believe what they were seeing.

But the inexperienced Bearcats were unable to close the deal. With 23.3 seconds left and UC still leading by one, Warren missed the front end of a one-and-one. With 12.6 seconds left, he fouled Devendorf as both players scrambled for a loose ball near mid-court. After UC called timeout, Devendorf made two free throws to give Syracuse a one-point lead.

Cincinnati then passed the ball inbounds to Warren, who passed to Sikes on the wing. Sikes passed to Vaughn, whose shot with time running out hit the front of the rim.

Final score: Syracuse 77, Cincinnati 76.

The Bearcats had suffered blowout losses to Ohio State and Memphis, they had lost to Wofford and UAB, but this was a crushing defeat that the Enquirer copy desk captured perfectly with the headline, "Orange Crusher," which I've borrowed for the title of this section.

"That's probably my worst memory from that season as far the games we played," Gentry said. "We had that win."

Sikes finished with a career-high 24 points. All of his points came on three-point field goals. Syracuse shot 60.7 percent in the first half, but only 38.1 percent in the second, and the Orange scored only 29 points after intermission. Cincinnati had five players in double figures and although the Bearcats shot only 36.4 percent from the field, they found a player with a hot hand and they rode it to within a whisker of a major upset. They even held their own on the boards, getting out-rebounded by only one.

The Bearcats were understandably devastated after the game, but perhaps they shouldn't have been. They were a missed free throw away from knocking off Syracuse after overcoming a 19-point deficit.

That resilience is what Cronin was trying to establish in his first year, but it didn't change the fact that the Bearcats were 0-3 in the Big East and had lost their last five games.

"That was tough," Cronin said, "because I knew it was going to be hard to get wins. I'm 35 years old and I'm coaching in the Carrier Dome. You grow up in the 80s as a kid watching Pearl Washington play in the Carrier Dome and here you are coaching your first game in the Dome. We were totally outmanned and we had them beat. Who knows (what it would have meant for the rest of the season to win that game)? It could have given us more confidence."

Sikes now says he wishes he had taken that last shot instead of passing to Vaughn.

"I really had a hot hand that game," Sikes said. "I was letting it fly. But you make sacrifices when you're part of something bigger."

After the game, the players and coaches stepped back into the frigid Syracuse weather. It was 13 degrees on that mid-January night, in other words just another winter night in the Cuse. They boarded their bus and headed for the airport knowing how close they had come to a major upset, only to have it snatched away in the final seconds.

"That really hurt because you hate to lose after overcoming a big deficit," Sikes said. "That leaves some hurt, some anger as well. But at the end of the day it's on to the next one. You feel that pain for a short time and then you try to focus on the next one. But that was a long, long plane ride back home, that's for sure."

——— MARCUS SIKES ———
Forward, Richmond, Virginia

'We were going to compete, that's just what we did'

When Sikes chose Cincinnati over Minnesota coming out of junior college, he wasn't expecting to play center. He was 6-foot-8 and 230 pounds and with his perimeter shooting ability was a fry cry from the kind of bruisers that manned the center position in the Big East.

At that point, Cronin was still expecting to have Hrycaniuk and Hall on his front line. After both were declared ineligible, Sikes was next in line for the five spot.

"It was demanding," he said, "but I didn't see it as a negative thing. I saw it as hey, if I'm going to get a lot of minutes playing the five, then this is my position. As long as I could stay on the court, this is what I'm going to do. Coach, you want me to play the five? OK, I'll do it. You want me to rebound and pick-and-roll for Deonta Vaughn? That's what I'm going to do. I'm going to play my role."

This was Sikes' second chance in Division I basketball and he was determined to make the most of it.

"I started at the University of Georgia," he said. "I spent two years there. I was a freshman and the bright lights and everything, I guess it kind of got to me. I had major minutes, playing in Rupp Arena, playing in big-time games.

"But I was just interested in playing and not the education part of it. I was skipping class and that got me in trouble there," Sikes said. "That led me to get suspended indefinitely from the team and I ended up transferring to junior college. I went to Indian Hills Community College."

Indian Hills is located in Ottumwa, Iowa, the hometown of MASH's Rader O'Reilly.

"I spent a few months there and then the coach got fired," Sikes said. "He placed me in Mt. San Jacinto in California. I played well there and Coach Davis reached out to me."

Davis had a relationship with Sikes' former AAU coach from when he was at Delaware.

"We were scouring the country for big guys, and at that time there were no big guys left," Davis said. "He was probably a little over his head when he first went to Georgia. His mindset probably wasn't right to be successful when he went there."

The decision to play at Cincinnati instead of Minnesota was easy for Sikes, mainly because he wanted to play in the Big East. The fact that it was the Bearcats who were looking for help made the situation even more attractive.

"When I was a young boy, it was cool to wear the Cincinnati

Bearcats shorts when you played basketball, with the 'C' on the side with the big claw," he said. "I identified with that as a kid."

Unlike Warren, who accepted Cronin's offer without visiting the Cincinnati campus, Sikes took an official visit. That's where he first met Cronin.

"It was a short, quick visit," Sikes said. "I think we went out to eat that night. He was a cool guy from the start. He kept it to a minimum. Basically he told me he was a new coach, he was coming from Murray State, and we were starting a new thing at Cincinnati. He said he had been here previously and that he had coached under some prestigious guys. He said, 'We're trying to build a program.'

"I asked him about playing time and he told me I'd have to compete for it. There were going to be several new guys here. No spots were guaranteed. Just come in and work your butt off.

"We just approached each game as it came. Practices were tough every day. We didn't have the mentality that this was going to be easy. We just went out and played. Coach instilled something in our minds not to concede to our opponents. We knew it was going to be tough. I was playing the five. John Williamson was playing the four. We were both about the same height, the same size. We had to try to be tougher than guys because obviously we weren't going to out-play teams in the Big East. We weren't more skilled than most teams in the Big East.

"You hate to lose. As far as the competing aspect, we were going to do that every night. No matter if we lost big or we just lost by a small margin, we were going to compete. That's just what we did."

Davis called Sikes "a functional dude. He shouldn't have been starting on a Big East team probably, but he was the best we had. I'll give Marcus credit. He bought in and did whatever we needed him to do. We needed him to rebound and defend inside and we needed him to try to score some buckets inside. He was really a face-up guy that could shoot. He was at a point in his career where he said, 'I'll do whatever you guys ask me to do.' "

Sikes had another memorable scoring game on January 27 against Georgetown at the Verizon Center in Washington, when he scored 19 points, making all five of his three-point shots, before fouling out with 13:19 left. The Bearcats trailed by only five midway through the second half, but an 11-3 Hoyas run sent Georgetown to an 82-67 victory.

Sikes was assigned to guard 7-foot-2, 270-pound Georgetown center Roy Hibbert, who was the 17th pick in the 2008 draft and played nine years in the NBA.

The Bearcats whittled a 17-point deficit to five at the half. They still were in contention even after Sikes departed, trailing by seven with 5:22 remaining. After the game, Sikes vented his frustration. "It's rough because a couple of their players are playing tough and physical, and then as soon as I want to be physical, there's a foul called," he said. "But that's how the game is played."

Sikes, from nearby Richmond, Virginia, had friends and family members on hand to watch him play, so to be forced out of the game so early, especially when he was playing so well, was hard for him to accept.

"My sister had just told me she was pregnant with my nephew," Sikes said. "It was an early (noon) game. I was playing against one of

Sikes scored 19 points at Georgetown before he fouled out.

my good friends, Patrick Ewing Jr. His dad is the coach there now. I used to love getting up for playing Georgetown.

"Once again the point guards were doing a good job of finding me. Coach said, 'Sikes, we're going to run you off some screens' because I think we had an injury at the three spot or something like that. We had practiced that for weeks. I was excited because I thought, yes, finally. Thank you, Coach. Give me some freedom. It worked out well and I was just letting it go. The shots happened to drop. Unfortunately, I got in some trouble guarding the big fella. It was one of those things where you're undersized guarding a big guy. It just didn't work out in our favor."

Said Cronin: "My question now is what the hell is he even doing in the game (with four fouls) with 13 minutes to go? There was nobody else to put in and that was the problem that whole year."

It's true that Cronin didn't have the depth to locate a quality replacement for Sikes at that point. But in this case that wasn't the reason he was still in the game with four fouls. When Sikes committed his fourth foul with 13:32 remaining, Cronin mistakenly thought the foul had been called on Vaughn. When he was told that the foul had been called on Sikes, he hurried to get him out of the game, but it was too late. Thirteen seconds later, he went to the bench with his fifth foul.

That season for Sikes was memorable for another reason. Around Thanksgiving, he learned that his mother had cancer, although his family tried to keep him from dwelling on it. She passed away in 2014.

"They didn't really tell me the gist of it because they wanted me to focus on what I was focusing on – finishing school, graduating, basketball," Sikes said, "because that can be kind of rough on a kid, so they kept it to a minimum. I was kind of in denial about the whole situation, like, oh, she'll get better. It's cool. She'll recover. We have faith in God. I was one of those guys who thought the best of every situation."

Sikes graduated in Spring, 2008 with a Bachelor of Science degree in Criminal Justice. He's single and works as an assistant coach at Trinity Valley College in Texas.

After he left Cincinnati, he played professionally in Brazil until he broke his ankle just before Christmas. He returned to the States to rehab, then signed to play in Cyprus. He also played in Lebanon, Turkey, Uruguay, Chile, Ecuador, and Argentina. And for the ABA Jacksonville Giants.

"I was so happy just to be a pro," he said, "and to continue playing. It's not NBA money, but it kept me well above water."

Sikes lived in Florida for a while and took care of his mom before she died. Then he called Cronin to find out how he could get into coaching.

"I would always keep in contact with Coach because we had a pretty good relationship," Sikes said. "He even sent flowers to my mom's funeral. I told him, 'I'm down here and I'm working with kids. I really want to get back into basketball of some sort.' I'm thinking he's going to say, 'Yeah, come on up, I've got a job for you in Cincinnati.' That's the way I imagined it going. But it didn't happen to go that way.

I was driving a fork lift for a company in Cincinnati for about six months. I got the job at Trinity at the end of '14. I've been here ever since.

"I love teaching the players what I know, correcting the same mistakes that I made when I was a young knucklehead. They do the same things. It's easy to identify and correct because you've been through it. I love recruiting. When you can sign a major guy to come play for you, that's like the best feeling in the world. I just want to have longevity in this career because it doesn't seem like work."

With Hrycaniuk eligible to play center, Sikes played a smaller role during his senior year than he had the previous season. He competed in all 32 games, but started only one, and that was on Senior Day. He played 15.6 minutes per game and averaged 3.9 points with 3.5 rebounds after starting 29 of 30 games as a junior and averaging 9.5 points with 5.0 rebounds in 29.3 minutes per game.

But that first season remains special to him.

"It had a big impact on me," he said. "It was my first year back at the Division I level. As a young guy, you kind of think differently than you do looking back at it. You kind of take it for what it's worth. OK, we had a bad season. We weren't as skilled as some of the other teams, but we did what we had to do regardless. It definitely played a big part in my life. You've got to learn how to deal with defeat and you still have to work hard going forward regardless.

"We're having a horrible season. So what? The next day we would still have practice. We still have to give 110 percent, regardless how the season is going. You cannot lay down just because it's not going the way you want it to. That's life. You have to deal with those things. It was such a brotherhood in the locker room. It was a special group. And we still talk to this day."

Now that the Bearcats are consistent winners and regular participants in the NCAA Tournament, Sikes can see what Cronin was trying to build back in 2006-07.

"I'm happy for the program in general," he said. "I'm an alumni and I guess you can say I take pride in that. I'm posting these things on my Instagram, No. 6 in the country, the highest ranking in Mick Cronin's era at Cincinnati. I'm proud to see how the program has evolved over the years and how Mick has turned it around. It's a beautiful thing. But it was expected. He does his work. He's a good coach. It just took time."

Chapter 13

A BREAK IN THE GLOOM

With the Bearcats mired in a five-game losing streak, Cincinnati's longest in 19 years, a fan in the student section brandished a sign in that read, 'Don't Stop Believing' as the players warmed up to face West Virginia on January 20 at Fifth Third Arena.

The sign seemed like an empty exhortation when the Mountaineers took a 17-point lead with 10:44 left in the first half. Whether or not the sign had anything to do with the resolve the Bearcats displayed for the rest of the game, the players acknowledged that they had noticed it after they delivered an unlikely 96-83 overtime victory against a team that entered the game with a 14-3 record, 4-2 in the Big East.

"If they believe, why shouldn't we?" Gentry said after the game.

Coming off the bench, Gentry - who was averaging only 5.5 points - played the game of his life. He made nine of 14 shots, including five of seven from three-point range. He also converted nine of 12 from the free throw line for a career-high 32 points that no one saw coming. Williamson also had a monster game with a double-double of 17 points and 13 rebounds. Five Bearcats scored in double figures.

"They played that 1-3-1, and Marv is one of the best corner

shooters to ever play at Cincinnati," Cronin said. "You let Marvin Gentry stand in the corner and he can shoot the lights out. We just kept running him on the baseline, getting him that corner jumper. And he kept making them."

In addition, Cincinnati out-rebounded West Virginia 44-32 and turned the ball over only six times against a team that had forced its opponents into an average of 19.6 turnovers with the unorthodox extended 1-3-1 zone the Mountaineers played under coach John Beilein.

Beilein left West Virginia at the end of the season to become the head coach at Michigan. His departure cleared the way for the return of Huggins, who was then at Kansas State, to coach at his alma mater, where he remains today.

Cincinnati, which trailed by 12 at halftime, took the lead at 60-58 on a McGowan dunk with 8:48 to go and led 71-66 with 4:02 left. With the score tied at 75-75, the Mountaineers had a chance to win in regulation when senior Frank Young tried to drive the baseline for a layup, but the Bearcats cut him off and he was forced to release a contested shot. Williamson rebounded with 0.4 seconds remaining.

Cronin called timeout to set up the final shot. Sikes threw a pass toward Gentry near the Cincinnati bench, but the pass was broken up. Cronin, who had already been called for one technical, ran onto the court, claiming that Gentry had been fouled. But he escaped a second technical that would have meant automatic ejection.

Williamson converted a three-point play on the Bearcats' first possession in overtime. After Young missed a three-point shot for

West Virginia, Vaughn knocked down a trey. When Williamson dunked with 2:47 remaining, Cincinnati held an 85-77 lead on the way to its first Big East victory under Cronin, before an energized crowd of 9,390.

The losing streak was over, and for a few days at least, the pressure was off the Bearcats, who avoided slipping to .500 for the first time that season.

"People have been awful nice around here with well-wishing and calls to hang in there, but you never accept losing no matter what the situation may be," Cronin said after the game. "You've got to find a way to fight harder, and the kids did that. It's a tough thing to ask them to do, what they're doing. We've just got to find a way to do it every night."

Finding a way to fight was never a problem for this team. The win over West Virginia marked the second time in as many games that they had overcome a first-half deficit of 17 points or more to take a lead late in the game. They were unable to prevail at Syracuse, but they got the job done at home against West Virginia.

There wasn't much time to celebrate, though. Next up on the schedule was a game at No. 9 Pittsburgh in four days. As Cronin used to say frequently when talking to reporters that season, "Welcome to the Big East."

—— MARVIN GENTRY ——
Guard, Fort Worth, Texas

'It prepared me to be a man'

The Cincinnati coaching staff didn't have a lot to sell when it recruited players during those first few seasons. The program was in shambles, the Bearcats played in an outdated arena, and they were at least several years away from being able to seriously consider the prospect of playing in the NCAA Tournament.

The coaches had two things going for them, though. One was the school's membership in the Big East, a magnet for recruits. The other – and perhaps most important – was the tradition and recent track record of success for the Bearcats under Huggins. Kids from all over the country had grown up watching Cincinnati play with a rough-and-tumble style that matched their fearsome black road uniforms, and these kids dreamed of playing there one day.

"That's one thing that Mick, being from Cincinnati, and previously coaching there, was big on, that we are the University of Cincinnati. We are the Bearcats," assistant coach Stubblefield said. "When you put that jersey on, you put it on with a lot of pride. It means something to put that jersey on. He definitely built on the name."

No one on Cronin's first team felt that pride more acutely than Gentry, who was a diehard Cincinnati fan growing up in Fort Worth. He loved to watch fellow Texan Kenyon Martin when he played for the Bearcats and was National Player of the Year in 2000. With Martin leading the way, Cincinnati was the nation's top-ranked team before he suffered a broken leg in the C-USA tournament. "He was down for the cause, whatever it took," Davis said of Gentry.

Gentry was playing at McLennan Community College in Waco,

For Gentry, a die-hard Cincinnati fan growing up in Fort Worth, playing for the Bearcats was a dream come true.

Texas, and he was being recruited to play for Cronin at Murray State when he heard that Cronin had landed the Cincinnati job.

"My coach called me," Gentry said. "He said, 'Mick wants to know if you want to go to Cincinnati.' I couldn't say yes quick enough. I had a lot of other choices, but there was no question at all that I would go to Cincinnati."

After he signed, Gentry drove to Cincinnati with a friend in a rented truck. As soon as they crossed the river into Ohio, they headed directly to the UC campus.

"When we walked into the gym, I walked out to mid-court because I had always seen the arena on TV," Gentry said. "I just took it all in. I stood there for 20 or 30 minutes. I was in awe. I was like a kid, really. I was so excited because I always wanted to play there and now I was going to. It was amazing."

Gentry's 32-point performance against West Virginia remains his greatest memory from his time at Cincinnati. He scored in double figures only seven more times during his two-year career. The closest he ever came to matching his total against the Mountaineers was a 22-point effort three games later against Louisville. He finished the season with a scoring average of 7.4 points, shooting 33.7 percent from long range.

He laughs when he recalls Cronin's reaction after his offensive outburst against the Mountaineers.

"He actually chewed me out, believe it or not," Gentry said, "because he was like, you're capable of having games like this all the time. You've just got to come to play. That was the best night of my life. That was the first time I had the fans at Fifth Third Arena chanting my name. It felt good, man, it felt really good. At the end, they were like 'Mar-vin Gen-try! Mar-vin Gen-try!' That was awesome. I had a ritual where I would throw my head band to the crowd, and they were waiting on it."

Before that game, Gentry had been bothered for most of the season with a sore wrist, the result of a fall he took while he was taking a charge.

"I really wasn't supposed to be playing, but I tried to tough it our for my teammates," he said. "I'd do anything I could to help us win. But it lingered. It was my shooting wrist so it made me have to adjust everything.

"By the West Virginia game I felt really good. It was an early (afternoon) game. We had shoot-around, and I normally would have gone back to my room. That day I stayed in the locker room and watched TV and lounged until we had to come back for the game. I told Tim Crowell that I feel different, like I'm about to have a breakout game. I really felt it."

Gentry averaged 15 points, five rebounds, five assists and three steals as a senior at Poly High School in Fort Worth, but the only scholarship offers he received were from mid-major schools. He thought he could do better than that so he sat out a year before enrolling at McLennan.

"I wanted to see which path I wanted to take in life," Gentry said. "I always wanted to play basketball, but I was undecided on my future. I was just lost as far as career-wise. I wanted to increase my market (value)."

Even after a successful junior college career – he was the North Texas Junior College Athletic Conference Player of the Year as a sophomore – Gentry appeared headed to a mid-major school. In this case, it was Murray State, But due to a stroke of good fortune, Huggins was fired by Cincinnati, Cronin secured the job, and Gentry's gamble to sit out a year paid off after all.

As thrilled as Gentry was to play at the school he had followed as a youngster, he had a difficult time adjusting to losing while he was at Cincinnati.

"I never really had a losing season until I got to UC," he said. "But we knew it was going to be an adjustment period. We pretty much had a whole new team. Most teams were returning five, six or seven guys so they had that cohesion. We had to build that.

"We left it on the floor, man. I don't think anyone felt we were overmatched. What happened is we would get a little fatigued because we had to play so hard. We were a bit undersized. We had a couple of guys that had to play out of position. We asked a lot of them. But no one ever complained. Whatever Coach said, we tried to do, and we tried to come out with a win.

"Every game was a challenge. If we lost on Monday and we've got a game on Wednesday, we were like, OK, how are we going to get better? How are we going to beat Pittsburgh? We just lost to Villanova. How are we going to beat Connecticut? We just kept trying to get better to get that next win. Coach Cronin would never allow us to (give up). If he felt like we were slacking, he'd run it out of us. If he wasn't going to be that way, he definitely wasn't going to allow us to be that way at all."

Gentry graduated in Spring, 2008 with a Bachelor of Science degree in Criminal Justice. He played professionally in Mexico and Venezuela for a few years before settling in Fort Worth where he's an elementary school teacher. He's married with four children, including two stepsons.

"Coach Cronin taught me to be prepared for anything that you do in life," Gentry said. "That's something that stuck with me. It prepared me to be a man. He did a great job off the court molding us to be better people. That was his main thing. It was always about life after basketball. Of course we were there to play basketball and get an education, but he always wanted us to make sure we were prepared after basketball. He did a great job staying in contact and keeping his word."

When I asked Gentry about his worst memories from that first season, he couldn't come up with any. In fact, the season was so special to him that he has the entire season, every game, recorded on DVR.

"Where the program is now," Gentry said, "I think we kind of laid the foundation of hard work and paved the way for the teams that were after us to get them to where Cincinnati basketball is now. I still feel like I'm a part of the team. (Last year) I thought they were going to the Final Four. That loss to Nevada (in the NCAA Tournament) was kind of tough to take. That hurt me like I was still part of the team."

Chapter 14

A NEW STREAK BEGINS

Four days after they knocked off West Virginia, the Bearcats were back in the Big East cauldron, facing No. 9 Pittsburgh at home. The Panthers would be the third ranked opponent for Cincinnati. The other two – Ohio State and Memphis – had hung lopsided losses on the Bearcats and in both cases they trailed by a wide margin in the first half – by 28 points against the Buckeyes and by 31 against the Tigers.

"We've got to start playing at the beginning of the game," Vaughn said before the Pitt game. "We still haven't figured that out yet. We've got to correct it."

The problem as Cronin saw it was that when the Bearcats started to fall behind, their inexperience flared up and they started rushing shots in an attempt to score in a hurry.

"It almost seems like it takes us a certain time to forget about the score and just play basketball," Cronin said. "Once we're able to do that, we start playing good basketball."

Against Pitt, Cincinnati fell behind again, trailing by 12 at halftime. But this time there would be no second-half recovery against the veteran Panthers, who started three seniors and a junior.

Five minutes into the game, Pitt reeled off 10 straight points. The Bearcats trailed 52-32 with 12:29 remaining, and lost 67-51 before 9,196 fans at Fifth Third Arena.

The Bearcats concentrated on containing Pitt center Aaron Gray by trapping him when the ball went to him in the low post, but Gray adeptly passed the ball back outside to open shooters. The Panthers made 12 of 19 shots from long range and shot 60.5 percent overall. Williamson led Cincinnati with 15 points and six rebounds.

Next up was the 82-67 loss at Georgetown in which Sikes scored 19 points before fouling out, dropping the Bearcats to 10-10 overall, 1-5 in the league.

On January 31, Cincinnati hosted Louisville, pitting Cronin against Pitino. Cincinnati had no answer for David Padgett, Louisville's 6-foot-11 center who scored 18 points on eight-of-10 shooting and pulled down 12 rebounds in a 69-53 Cardinals win. Gentry scored 22 for the Bearcats, giving him an average of 18 points over his last four games.

"I'm getting back to my normal self," Gentry said. "To everybody else, it's looking new, but I'm just getting back in rhythm."

After the game, Pitino offered a note of encouragement to Cincinnati fans who were suffering right along with the players.

"It's going to take Mick time," Pitino said. "It's not going to happen overnight, but the same results he had at Murray State will happen here. And once he gets there, we'll both be there together. He'll get you there, without question, without a shadow of doubt."

Right around that time, Cronin welcomed some good news about the academic performances of his players during Fall quarter. The news might not have meant much to fans who care only about winning, but given the academic condition of the program when

Cronin took over, it was viewed by athletic department officials as a crucial step forward.

The school announced that the men's basketball team had posted a 2.75 grade-point average, a half-point better than the previous year's team during the same period. Sikes and Miller both made the Dean's List.

Next to the win over Xavier, the announcement might have been the high point of the season for the Bearcats, even though it received little attention.

"Our guys are working hard doing a great job on campus representing our program academically and socially," Cronin said. "And they're playing hard between the lines, fighting hard to get better every day."

But the losses kept coming. On February 4, the Bearcats lost at home to St. John's, 73-64, which won its first conference road game of the season. The Bearcats shot 33.3 percent, and made only 8 of 30 three-point attempts, falling to 1-7 in the league. The Red Storm made 26 of 32 foul shots compared with 16 of 27 for the Bearcats.

After the game, Cronin praised his team's effort, only to lament its inability to make shots.

"The tough thing is we've had games where we shot the ball extremely well," he said, "like at Georgetown. But because we're totally outmanned, no matter how well we shot it, we probably weren't going to win. Where if we shoot the ball that well today, it's a whole different story."

In a season filled with excruciating losses, the Bearcats' 71-70 loss at Providence on February 6 was near the top of the list, although after a while it became difficult to distinguish one loss from another. The Bearcats were on the verge of their second Big East victory of the season when they led, 70-62, with 1:41 left at Dunkin' Donuts Center in downtown Providence, but they still found a way to lose.

Cronin was furious, maybe as angry as he was after any game all season. The game-winning points came on a three-point play by Sharaud Curry, who led the Friars with 24 points. Curry penetrated the lane and made a jump shot while getting fouled by Vaughn. After he made the free throw that gave Providence a one-point lead, Williamson shot what would have been the game-winning basket, but it rimmed out as time expired.

During the final 1:41, the Bearcats were outscored, 9-0. They missed the front end of the one-and-one bonus twice, committed an over-and-back violation, and instead of backing the ball out to eat the clock, McGowan tried to make a layup over 6-foot-10 Providence center Herbert Hill with 21.7 seconds left.

"That was brutal," Cronin said. "That one I took really hard. We threw the ball in bounds and Cedric should have dribbled it out. He tried to lay it in and Herbert Hill blocked in from behind. If you don't have a clean layup, you've got to dribble it out, and we didn't dribble it out. Again, we were outmanned at every position and still had the game won.

"It would have been great for the kids to experience a victory. The competitor in me got pissed after the game, but then the next day you realize your kids really needed it just from a morale standpoint."

McGowan didn't start for the first time all season. He would start only three of the Bearcats' final eight games. Cronin chose instead to go with a three-guard starting lineup with Gentry, Vaughn Warren. When McGowan did enter the game he played power forward instead of the small forward position he had played most of the season.

The Bearcats narrowly missed another road victory in their next game – at Rutgers on February 10. Again, they were unable to hold a lead in the closing minutes, squandering a 67-61 edge with 4:04 to play. The Scarlet Knights outscored them 12-2 the rest of the game, including nine unanswered points, to walk away with a 73-69 victory. Cincinnati was outscored 26-7 at the free throw line.

Warren, who scored 13 points, missed the Bearcats' final two shots. As he walked to the locker room in the Louis Brown Athletic Center, he said, "If this was a bridge, I would keep walking."

"I feel sick," he said later. "I don't want to sound cocky, but man, we're supposed to be winning more than this. It's just the little things that we do. It's not working."

There was no late-game angst for the Bearcats in their next game, at Villanova. They were thoroughly beaten, 64-48, by a much better team that limited them to 13 field goals. They trailed by 17 at the half and absorbed their seventh straight loss and 12th in their last 13 games.

"We got a lesson tonight in how to play hard," Cronin said after the game. "It was a learning experience. We need to become who they are. There's a team that knows how to play hard."

On February 17, the day before the Bearcats were scheduled to play Notre Dame at home, Mike Williams, a former McDonald's All-

American who had transferred from Texas and was sitting out the season under the NCAA's transfer rules, got some bad news from home.

——— MIKE WILLIAMS ———
Forward, Camden, Alabama

'It hit hard, man'

As he was walking back to his dorm after practice on February 17, Williams noticed a message on his phone from his mother asking him to call her.

"They didn't tell me what happened," Williams said. "They just told me to call them as soon as I could. Once I got done with everything and got situated, I called them and they told me the news."

The Williams family home in Camden, Ala., had burned to the ground. Everything inside had been destroyed.

"It hit hard, man," Williams said, "because at the time you're still a college student. You're not making money yet. For my family to go through that situation when they're struggling and there's basically nothing I can do about it. The right thing to do was to just stay in school and get an education.

"My family, we were all close. We were raised that way. We were raised God first and family is after God, so for me to not be there for them to come and see with my own eyes that everybody is OK, that was tough. But being at such a great school, with great fans and great people in the community, they all came together and they had a fundraiser for myself and for my family and they raised a lot of money to help with the situation. That was a great help.

"You don't wish that to happen, but if it were to happen, I wish it could have happened a few years later because I would have been playing professional basketball and I would have been able to help them with their needs."

Fortunately, no one was hurt. Williams' parents, Alice and Michael Gladney, weren't home at the time of the fire. Neither was his brother, Derrick, 24; or his sister Jamiah, 4. The only family member who was home was Williams' 15-year-old brother Demetric, who was sleeping when the fire broke out but was awakened by a smoke alarm and escaped the house unharmed.

Because of his status as a McDonald's All-American, when Williams committed to Cincinnati in late May 2006, he infused the program with credibility at a time when it was most needed. As a senior at Wilcox Central High School, he was rated the No. 18 prospect in the country by TheInsiderHoops.com. He had averaged 2.3 points and 3.1 rebounds at Texas the year before and was an Academic All-Big 12 second-team selection.

Williams knew about the situation he would face at Cincinnati, but chose to go anyway.

"I came because back in my high school days, Mick was recruiting me," Williams said. "The head person on my AAU team knew Mick, so I always knew him. We ended up reconnecting and I ended up at Cincinnati. Mick was trying to get everything started for himself as well there. Coming back home and coaching there was a big opportunity for him. I knew that he wanted to bring in some guys that could help him re-start everything and change the image of the program."

Williams couldn't play in games that year, nor could he travel to road games. But he could practice.

"I did everything with the guys and they were seeing what I could bring to the team," Williams said. "I knew 100 percent that I could help them, but I wasn't able to at the moment. That

Mike Williams playing for the Bearcats in 2008-09.

was tough for myself, my teammates, the coaching staff, the whole program.

"I came to practice and I continued to work hard, leading by example, being a leader in the locker room and just bringing them positive support, just continue to cheer the guys on. Of course, it was going to wear on them, and it did, but we showed great character. We stayed together as a team. We were able to stay strong. That was a tough season, but our team was so close and we all got along so well, that we always had each other's back and we stood together. We didn't go our separate ways or pointing fingers."

Williams, a 6-foot-7, 240-pound forward, was itching to make an impact on the court in 2007-08, but never got the chance. About a month before the season began, he suffered a torn Achilles tendon, which forced him to miss another season. He returned to play in 2008-09 and started 28 of the Bearcats' 29 games, averaging 9.8 points and 5.7 rebounds. He graduated in Summer, 2009 with a Bachelor of Science degree in Criminal Justice and then headed off to play professionally overseas. Before he retired in December 2017, he had played in Canada, Mexico. Argentina and Portugal. He was living in Pensacola, Florida, when I interviewed him, but he was getting ready to move to Texas.

He didn't make the impact that he and Cronin hoped he would when he signed with the Bearcats, but his stay in Cincinnati was memorable for another reason.

"I met my wife there," he said. "We've been married since 2009. We have three beautiful kids, two daughters and a son. I met her a month after being there. She's from Georgia. She played on the women's team."

Her maiden name is Emy Ogide. She was a forward from Rockmart, Ga., who wore No. 14.

"Me and Marvin Gentry, we were like two peas in a pod," Williams said. "We were hanging out outside the dorm and she was moving in. We passed a few words and I held the door open for her so she could move more of her stuff in. I saw her a few days later when we were washing clothes. We had a conversation, and the rest is history."

Williams credits Emy with helping him get through the difficult times he experienced at Cincinnati.

"I went through a struggle," he said. "But she's a strong woman. I really leaned on her for that support and she delivered. She's my best friend. I look back at my time at Cincinnati just like I do at every other experience in life. You can learn from everything no matter where you're at - what state, what country, what city - the things we you go through help form us into the person that we are today. It's best to take the good and the bad. Take the good things and cherish it and let it blossom, and the bad things, you learn from it and turn those bad things into good."

CHAPTER 15

THE END IS NEAR

On February 19, the Bearcats lost to Notre Dame, 76-64, before 11,038 fans at Fifth Third Arena, but there were encouraging performances from Williamson (23 points and nine rebounds) and Vaughn (22 points). On a team with no choice but to look to the future, such positive signs were golden.

"I'm just trying to finish up strong," Williamson said after the game. "I'm not going to let the season go. I'm not going to give up.'

"You've got to give him credit," Cronin said. "The Big East kind of hit him in the face when Big East play started. But he's found a way to jump-start himself. You know what they say, you either toughen up or go home. And he's toughened up."

Still the Bearcats' record slipped to 10-16, which assured them of their first losing season since 1987-88. At that point, they had lost eight straight and 13 of their last 14.

No. 12 Georgetown was up next, this time in Cincinnati, and the Hoyas posted a 75-65 victory. Again Williamson and Vaughn led the way for the Bearcats, with Williamson scoring 15 and Vaughn getting 19. Cincinnati out-rebounded Georgetown 31-27 but shot only 39.7 percent from the field compared with Georgetown's 54.2 percent.

The Bearcats played well, but it didn't matter.

"There are two things you have to do in this league to be successful," Cronin said. "You've got to be able to fight hard and compete because every game is a battle royal. We passed that test with flying colors tonight. This is the hardest we've competed in a while."

The Bearcats committed 11 first-half turnovers, which put them in a six-point hole, even though they twice led by 10 points in the first half. They trailed by only three with 12:17 left and by seven with 7:09 to go, but could get no closer, falling to 10-17 overall, 1-12 in the Big East. The loss eliminated the Bearcats from qualifying for the Big East tournament, in the days when only 14 of the league's 16 teams qualified.

Timmy Crowell made his first start of the season at point guard, in place of Warren. He scored five points and pulled down five rebounds, with two assists, in 22 minutes.

"I just thought he deserved to start," Cronin said after the game. "His understanding of our zone is probably the best of all the guards. I thought he played very solid."

After the game, John Thompson III, the Hoyas' head coach, praised Cronin and his players for their effort under overwhelming odds.

"Mick's teams have always played hard," Thompson said. "You know you're going to be in a dogfight when you play against them. We're extremely fortunate to be getting out of here with a win."

Cincinnati's effort wasn't nearly as praiseworthy in its 58-45 loss at DePaul on February 24. The Bearcats committed 20 turnovers, shot only 33.3 percent from the field, and generally played as if they couldn't wait for the long, debilitating season to end. They made only two of 13 three-point shots.

Timmy Crowell transferred to Fort Lewis College in Colorado after playing one season at Cincinnati.

Crowell started again, but this time didn't play so well, committing five turnovers in 13 minutes.

"That was our worst game yet," Warren said.

"We stunk up the gym the whole night," Sikes said.

"You're asking kids to overachieve every night,"

Cronin said.

The loss was Cincinnati's 10th straight, the school's longest losing streak since the 1924-25 team lost 11 in a row.

The Bearcats had one more win in them, which they saved for Senior Night at Fifth Third Arena against Seton Hall. Both Cincinnati seniors – McGowan and Allen – started in their final game before 8,019 fans.

Their second lengthy losing streak of the season came to an end with a 70-67 overtime victory, which eliminated the Pirates from the Big East tournament. Cincinnati had a chance to win in regulation, but Vaughn turned the ball over. He made up for that miscue by hitting a trey in OT that gave the Bearcats the lead for good. Warren, who scored 13 points with five rebounds and only one turnover in 45 minutes, made one of two free throws with 7.6 seconds left to give Cincinnati a three-point lead. A three-point shot by Seton Hall's Larry Davis fell short, and the Bearcats had their second Big East win of the season.

"It's great for the kids," Cronin said after the game. "Put yourself in their situation. I've said many times I plan on being here for 20 years. I'm trying to build something brick by brick. But for the kids in the locker room it means a lot to them to be able to get a win and feel good about themselves."

There was one more game to go, on Saturday March 3 against West Virginia in Morgantown, against a Mountaineer team the Bearcats had already beaten. But there would be no two-game winning streak to finish Cronin's first season.

This time Cincinnati played without Gentry, who had scored 32 points against the Mountaineers in that first game. He had been playing for several games with plantar fasciitis, which also caused him to miss the Seton Hall game.

The Mountaineers made 14 of 28 shots from beyond the arc and converted 17 of 21 free throws. They led by 15 at halftime and coasted to the victory, 79-65.

While most Division I players across the country were getting ready to play in their conference tournaments, the Bearcats were finished for the season.

"You know what this season makes you want to do?" Warren said. "It makes you want to live in the gym."

When Cronin emerged from the locker room at WVU Coliseum after talking to his players, he looked at me and said, "I'll bet you're tired of watching this."

Then he promised that the Bearcats would "be exponentially better next season. It will be a completely different look next year. Now, are we going to win the Big East next year? No. It's a process. But at least we'll have 12 or 13 guys on scholarship with some size and some quickness where you can start to implement your style of play. That's what I'm looking forward to, not playing from behind the 8-ball."

Cronin now realizes that when the end came it was merciful.

"It was like enough's enough," he said. "I knew the guys had nothing left in them, so it was almost like it was good for all of us. It was over. We gave it everything we had. We fought to the end. Even in that game, we fought as hard as we could. It wasn't like, well, I'm glad it's over in the sense that I don't like my team. It was for my team. I was glad they didn't have to deal with it anymore."

McGowan and Allen had played in their last college games. So had Barwin, who went back to being a full-time football player. Crowell, who played 15 minutes against West Virginia, didn't know as he walked to the bus that he, too, had played his last game for the Bearcats.

——— TIMMY CROWELL ———
Guard, Albuquerque, New Mexico

'I just didn't feel the same as a player'

In April 2006, on the day before Crowell had planned to announce publicly that he had verbally committed to Purdue, he got a call from Cronin, who offered him a chance to play at Cincinnati.

"I chose that over Purdue real quick," Crowell said. "I pretty much just loved the environment at Cincinnati. It was like Bearcat Nation. It had that long-standing history. To be a part of that was just amazing. When I was growing up I always liked how aggressive they were. They just had an aura about them. They had the Jordan logo. Everything about them made them one of those teams that I felt like if I ever played for them I'd be like a junkyard dog. It was a dream, man. When I came out to the city, I felt love. It was the big time. It was the big show. That's where I wanted to be."

Crowell, a 6-foot-2, 170-pound point guard from Albuquerque, N.M., was coming off a senior year at Midland College in Texas, in which he averaged 11.0 points with 7.5 assists and was a first-team all-conference selection."

"I thought I was walking in to be the starting point guard," Crowell said.

But that's not how it worked out. Vaughn and Warren both outplayed him and Crowell, was limited to spot duty.

When Crowell signed, Cronin described him as "a pass-first guy, but he's a capable scorer as well. He can knock down the open shot."

Crowell played in all 30 games, but started only two, averaging 9.7 minutes, 1.5 points and 0.8 assists. He never felt connected to Cronin the way he had with his previous coaches.

"I didn't feel like I could catch the flow of the game of what he wanted or what he needed," Crowell said. "It was like I was just trying to stop a leak. I didn't feel like I was there to be utilized. I just didn't feel the same as a player, so I wasn't as aggressive. But I don't think that was anybody's fault."

When Vaughn emerged as the Bearcats' best offensive player, with Warren manning the point, and with Gentry coming into his own as a scorer after his wrist healed, there simply weren't enough minutes to go around.

"I could see how much easier it was for other guys like John Williamson," Crowell said. "He was just like a freak amazing athlete. The game at that level was coming easier for him. I could see the game as I wanted to play it, but I had a hard time at that level. I don't think I was ever overmatched. If anything, the coaches and my teammates encouraged me to shoot and be more aggressive. It was just that I had something that was holding me back when the lights came on."

Crowell wasn't unhappy. Aside from the fact that he wasn't playing as much as he had hoped, he was enjoying his experience at Cincinnati.

"We knew that everybody wanted the same thing," Crowell said. "but we didn't have all the pieces to the puzzle. We were a junior college team coming together, a junior college all-star team. We had amazing guys that had amazing talent. I think we knew we were in it together. I don't think we ever gave up on each other. That's the one thing that I loved about it."

But as the season wore on, as the losses piled up and as the minutes for Crowell continued to be hard to come by, he felt drained.

"It was the first time ever that I was involved in a losing season," he said. "When you're winning, you always have a little more motivation to keep going and keep working harder. When you're consistently in the gym with your body getting beat up, it was new for me to work out like that. It was somewhere between D-I and NBA workouts. It was like, what am I doing this for?

"We had some amazing bonds with the staff. There were some alumni from past years. They tried to pour the environment into us, the culture. We learned how serious the game was. It don't matter how small you are in height or how big. We were running through a wall. We were big dogs. We were Bearcats."

Crowell wouldn't be a Bearcat for long. Shortly after the season ended, he was called into Davis' office.

"He told me, 'I don't think it's going to work out for you because we're bringing in some new talent and we don't think you're going to get much playing time,' " Crowell said. "The conversation started like I had a choice, but I knew it wasn't a choice."

Crowell hadn't seen it coming.

"To be honest with you," he said, "I don't think I ever expressed this to many people, but I sat in that office crying and begging for my spot. I told them I didn't care if I was just on the bench, I want to be here and I want to finish as a Bearcat. That's all that matters to me."

Crowell walked out of Davis' office and headed back to his room. He told Gentry and Vaughn what had just happened, that his scholarship would not be renewed for the following season. Then he want upstairs and told Sikes, Hrycaniuk and Williams.

"They were like looking at me like I was crazy," Crowell said, "like you've got to kidding."

"The truth of it is that the level was too high for him," Cronin said.

Crowell transferred to Fort Lewis College, a Division II school in Durango, Colo., where he averaged 12.2 points and 6.9 assists in 2007-08, helping the Skyhawks win the Rocky Mountain Athletic Conference regular-season and tournament championships on the nation's second-ranked team.

"I felt like I got my juice back," Crowell said. "Bob Hoffman was an amazing coach. He let me be me. He always asked me, when you were at Cincinnati, what would you do in this situation? How did you guys work out? They took me right in and let me know that it's your show. The fans were chanting my name. It was amazing. It was because I had Cincinnati on my resume."

After his finished his senior year at Fort Lewis, Crowell played professionally in Chile, Lithuania, Alaska and Mexico. He's single and lives in Orlando, Fla., where he works for Holiday Inn Club Vacations. He has a daughter who lives with her mother in Cincinnati.

Crowell didn't get to play as much at Cincinnati as he hoped. And he certainly didn't leave on a positive note, but he said the experience had a positive impact on his life.

"I had very bitter moments," he said, "bitter and depressing, but it taught me where my dedication was, where my push was, where my drive was. It brought a whole 'nother light to me, the dedication that he was requesting from us – day in and day out at 6 o'clock in the morning, sometimes 9 p.m. You didn't have a life as a college student, but you learned a lot of responsibility. It was the big time. He wanted to be in the big time and he wanted us to perform that way. I wouldn't trade it for anything else in the world."

CHAPTER 16

'WE'VE COME A LONG WAY'

When Cronin took over at Cincinnati, there were no instructions to help guide him in rebuilding a program already on academic probation, with only one true scholarship player and an angry fan base.

There was really no one he could turn to for advice about how to deal with a rebuilding process like the one he faced. His two college coaching mentors were Huggins and Pitino. Huggins had been through a rebuilding process of his own at Cincinnati in 1989, but he started with four quality scholarship players that he inherited from the Tony Yates era. Besides, he had recently been fired, so it was unlikely that he would provide assistance to the school that had just forced him out.

Pitino took over a desolate situation at Kentucky in 1989, with the Wildcats on NCAA probation, but he started with five experienced scholarship players, which would have seemed like an embarrassment of riches to Cronin. Nonetheless, Pitino was the best resource he had. Even that was awkward, though, because he had to compete against Pitino, who was coaching at Louisville in the Big East. That didn't stop Pitino from offering him encouragement, which Cronin was happy to have.

"He would always tell me, you don't want to win too much your first year," Cronin said. "You want to get better every year. I said,

'Well, you don't have to worry about that.' "

Cronin was as prepared as anyone could have expected, given the situation. He had a semblance of a plan in that he knew he had to start with mostly junior college players. And he had a list of the ones he thought he could get to make his first team at least representative, if not fully competitive in the Big East.

The Bearcats worked to lay the foundation that would make the Cincinnati program a success in later years.

Of course he wanted to win as many games as he could, but he knew there were limits to how much he could accomplish in that regard. There were no limits, though, on what he could do to establish what he wanted his program to be moving forward.

"That was my big thing," he said. "If I'm a fan or if I'm the administration, I want to know a) does this guy know how to give his team a chance to win with his coaching? and b) how hard do his guys play regardless of the situation? That's what I tried to stay focused on.

"The one thing I learned being around winning teams prior to that is, you could tell when other teams have given up. You could kind of hear their players mumbling late in February. You could kind of see it. You just can't let that happen. And then you hope that people notice, hey, these guys never give in. That's who we're going to be. That was my goal. We have to set that tone so when we do get good enough that's what we're about."

When a team loses a close game to a more highly-ranked and obviously more talented team, the coach is supposed to proclaim that he doesn't believe in moral victories. But with only two conference victories in his first season, Cronin had no choice but to embrace a close loss as a success. He didn't see that as accepting defeat.

"There were games when you'd lose by 10 and you'd think we should have lost by 30," he said. "But we only lost by 10 because of how hard these guys were playing and my game plan. That keeps you going. You know that you didn't win, but you really did."

Still, losing wore on him. How could it not? Losing so much and being so continually overmatched would wear on anyone who's competitive. And Cronin is ultra-competitive. Plus he had risen through the coaching ranks in winning programs like Cincinnati and Louisville. Losing was foreign to him.

During those times when he was frustrated, Cronin tried not to let his players see it. That was also part of the plan he formulated as he went along.

"That's the number one thing in leadership," he said. "You've got to give off an air of confidence. Everybody's watching you so when you walk into practice you've got to walk in there like, hey, we're going to win the next game. That's just how you've got to be. You've got no chance if you let results get you down, if you let bad breaks get you down. Everybody's looking to you, especially young people, so if you come in there ready to go, then they think, hey, this guy ain't giving up, so I ain't giving up."

But there were some days when they could sense his frustration, no matter how hard he tried to hide it. The important thing for them was how he handled it.

"Mick was frustrated for sure," Williamson said. "I don't think he was discouraged, though, because he has that mind, which is where I think I got it from, that mind that you're not going to discourage me. That has sustained me. It made me work harder. Mick really wanted us to win. He wanted us to reap what we were putting in. We all were frustrated for losing, but I don't think we were frustrated or upset at the work we were putting in to get the win." There was plenty of frustration, though, among the fans, some of whom believed, against the evidence, that there was no reason the Bearcats shouldn't keep winning the way Kennedy had the year before and the way Huggins did for 16 years. They were still upset over the Huggins' firing and the fact that Kennedy wasn't hired to succeed him. Home attendance dropped.

The Bearcats averaged 8,831 fans in a 13,176-seat arena in

Cronin's first season, down from 9,301 the previous year under Kennedy and 11,059 in Huggins' final season. Most of the fans who showed up were supportive, but some were visibly not in Cronin's corner.

"I was a little shocked when people would hold signs up to get rid of Mick," said Cronin's dad, Hep. "I would think, don't they understand? And they didn't. They did not understand and it shocked me how stupid they were, what he had to go through just to field a team.

"He would never admit it, but it bothered him a little bit. He was worried about his job. I think he saw the light at the end of the tunnel if he could just survive, that he was going to be able to get players, but it was going to take three or four years to get to 20 wins. Even when we were showing improvement, people kept it up. I would think, can't they see the progress, that we are now competitive? The more they held up signs it just motivated him more. He kept it a lot inside. It wasn't easy, but he kept most of it inside."

This was another instance where Pitino advised him. In fact, he predicted how the fans would react based on his own experience. You're not Huggins, he told Cronin, and because of that you should expect to attract criticism, fair or not.

"He said there were going to be some people who, until their death were going to say it's not the same because you're not him," Cronin said. "I don't take it personal. There's a lot of guys in my business that have a lot of talent that haven't survived because they've cared too much about what people say or think about them. It gets them down. If you let it affect you, it's going to affect your staff, your players. If that's what's taking up your thoughts, it's going to get you eventually.

"Maybe it has made me more hardened, I don't know. I've never analyzed it. My dad will tell you I was always this way growing up. I was always a guy that was going to do what I thought was right or what I thought needed to be done. It wasn't easy. There would be times when I would say, 'Hey, I'm not the one who wrecked the program. I'm here to fix it.' "

Cronin tried to focus on the fans who did show up, the ones who were supportive and wanted what was best for the program, the ones who asked what they could do to help.

"If it wasn't for them, there would have been no more program," he said. "Those are the people I'm still closest with now in our world of UCATS (Cincinnati's athletics boosters organization). I'll never forget those people."

Instead of worrying about disgruntled fans, Cronin concentrated on his players and guarded against their getting so discouraged that they gave up. Occasionally, though, he would make the mistake of pushing them too hard with longer and longer practices. That's where Davis stepped in.

Davis had been in a rebuilding situation as the head coach at Furman and he understood that sometimes the wise thing to do is to pull back a little on how hard you work your players.

"I would tell him sometimes, they're only capable of so much," Davis said. "We can't get this guy to be that much better of a ball-handler by keeping him an extra hour. They're not going to defend that much better. We've got to give them fresh legs. And he listened."

Despite all the problems he faced, Cronin had the benefit of players who worked had, were coachable and who cared.

"You have to know that you have to just keep on pounding nails," Davis said. "Mick used to use that term. What people don't understand is that when you're at this level it's hard in one or even two years to go from here to there, because players are looking at you like, you're not very good, I'm not going to go there."

Cronin promised things would get better in 2007-08 and he was right to an extent. The Bearcats went from 11-19 to 13-19 overall and from two Big East wins to eight, which moved them up to 10th place. They knocked off Louisville at Freedom Hall, beat No. 15 Pitt at Fifth Third Arena and blew out West Virginia in its first season under Huggins, 62-39, in Morgantown. At the end of the regular season they were invited to play in the inaugural College Basketball Invitational, where they lost to Bradley, 70-67, in Peoria, Ill.

On April 16, a few weeks after the season ended, Cronin pulled off a huge coup when 6-foot-9 forward Yancy Gates, a first-team all-state selection and Top 25 national recruit from Cincinnati's Withrow High School, announced that he planned to attend Cincinnati in 2008-09. He chose the Bearcats over Ohio State and Georgetown, among many others.

"You've got to be able to keep the best player in your city," Cronin said when Gates signed in November. Point guard Cashmere Wright, another top recruit, signed as part of the same class. Gates finished his college career with 1,485 points, which ranks 15th in school history, and 916 rebounds, which ranks 10th. Wright scored 1,317 points (tied for 23rd) and 482 assists (fourth).

The Bearcats produced their first winning season under Cronin in 2008-09, going 18-14 overall, 8-10 in the Big East, but ended their season with a loss to DePaul in the first round of the Big East Tournament. That was followed by another recruiting coup, the signing of Lance Stephenson, a McDonald's high school All-American. Stephenson was the leading scorer in the history of New York state, and a top 15 recruit nationally.

With Vaughn, Gates and Stephenson leading the way, the Bearcats went 19-16, 7-11 in the Big East in 2009-10, and played in the NIT, where they lost at home to Dayton in the second round. Stephenson, who was named the Big East Rookie of the Year, left after one season and was taken by the Indiana Pacers in the second round of the NBA draft with the 40th overall pick to become the first UC player to be drafted in the Cronin coaching era.

The Bearcats had their breakthrough year in 2010-11, when they posted a 26-9 record, went 11-7 in the Big East, and played in their first NCAA Tournament, in Cronin's fifth year at Cincinnati. They beat Missouri in the first round before losing to eventual national champion Connecticut by 11 in the second. They've been to the Big Dance every year since, advancing to the Sweet 16 in 2011-12.

When the Big East broke up after the 2012-13 season, Cincinnati became a charter member of the American Athletic Conference. The Bearcats went 27-7, 15-3 in the league, and shared the first AAC title with Louisville, which left the following year for the Atlantic Coast Conference, and Cronin was named the conference Coach of the Year. Cincinnati's Sean Kilpatrick led the league in scoring with an average of 20.6 points and became the first Bearcat to receive first-team Associated Press All-American recognition since Steve Logan in 2002. He also became the second player in school history to score 2,000 career points, finishing with 2,145, second only to the legendary Oscar Robertson's 2,973.

The Bearcats went 30-6 in 2016-17 and 31-5 in 2017-18, tying the school record for victories. They won the AAC regular-season and tournament titles, and senior forward Gary Clark was named conference Player of the Year. Cronin was The Sporting News Coach of the Year; and junior forward Jacob Evans III was drafted by the NBA champion Golden State Warriors, in the first round with the 28th overall pick, becoming the first Cronin recruit at Cincinnati to get drafted in the first round.

Early that season, the Bearcats travelled to Los Angeles and posted a 77-63 victory in historic Pauley Pavilion over UCLA, with its 11 national titles and the rich legacy of Lew Alcindor, Bill Walton, John Wooden and so many more. By then I was writing for Cincinnati's athletics web site and was still traveling with the team. As I boarded the plane for the charter flight back to Cincinnati, I passed Cronin sitting next to his dad in the front of the plane, basking in the glow of the win.

Before I sat down, he called me back to his seat.

"We've come a long way, haven't we?" he said.

I told him that he surely had come a long way and that after what he had been through his first few years, he deserved to savor the moment. I asked him later why the win over UCLA was so satisfying to him, considering that by then he had coached his team to plenty of noteworthy wins, including a Sweet 16 appearance in 2012.

"I mean, it's UCLA," he said, "beating up on the Bruins in Pauley Pavilion. You're sitting there thinking back to being at Memphis. The thing about it for me is it gives you a reference. Some guys have lived in Camelot. It gives me a lot of perspective."

Cronin has survived the fans' anger and their doubts about his ability to turn the program back into a winner without the arrests and the poor APR. Along the way, he suffered an arterial dissection in his brain that caused him to miss most of the 2014-15 season and he flirted with leaving his alma mater to become the head coach at Nevada, Las Vegas. In the end, he decided to stay home where he could be close to his dad, who travelled to all the road games with him, and his proud West Side Cincinnati roots.

Cronin knows there's still more work to do. His Bearcats have yet to advance past the Sweet 16 after suffering a devastating loss last year in the second round of the 2017-18 NCAA Tournament, when they squandered a 22-lead with 11:37 remaining and fell to Nevada 75-73 in the second-largest comeback in NCAA Tournament history. It hurt more because that team was undoubtedly his most talented Cincinnati team, the one with the best chance to make a deep run in the tournament.

"I'll never get over that," Cronin told reporters a few weeks later at the team banquet. "My responsibility is different than most coaches. Very few people are coaching at their alma mater and in their hometown and grew up a Bearcat fan, where their father was a varsity letter winner and their mother grew up on campus.

"My responsibility and the weight of that is on me...I can't possibly express it to you, how much I bear that burden of getting back to a Final Four. But you've just got to move on. You never get over it."

As he entered his 13th season, Cronin ranked second on Cincinnati's all-time wins list for coaches with a record of 268-140. He needs 132 wins to pass Huggins, who left with a record of 399-127 in 16 years. The Bearcats have made eight straight NCAA Tournament appearances, joining Kansas, Duke, Michigan State, Gonzaga and North Carolina as the only schools that can match that record of consistency. On the academic front, twenty-one of Cincinnati's last 24 seniors have graduated since 2011-12, including the last 12.

Kennedy, the people's choice to succeed Huggins on a permanent basis, resigned on February 18, 2018 after 12 years at Ole Miss. The Rebels, who completed the season under an interim head coach, finished 11-16 overall, 4-10 in the Southeastern Conference. Kennedy was 245-156 at Ole Miss, making him the school's career leader in victories. His teams won 20 games nine times and made NCAA appearances in 2013 and 2015, six fewer than Cronin's Cincinnati teams have played in.

There was no way to predict after going 11-19 in 2006-07 that the Bearcats would eventually join a group of elite programs with eight straight NCAA Tournament appearances. The players on that team didn't think in those terms. They were more focused on getting through each game and finishing the season.

But now, years after they've left, they look back and see what it was all about. They understand why Cronin coached them the way he did and see the impact that season had on their lives. And they can see that it was all worth it when they watch the current Bearcats play.

"When I watch them play, I feel like that's me," Warren said. "Not to say that I made this or I built this, I'm not like that, not by myself. But I was a key part to building that program … When I watch them now, I feel like that's what we were trying to build. Now look, they're going to the tournament every year."

That's music to Cronin's ears.

"I want them to realize that we would have never got there without them," he said. "I just feel like they always need to know that. It always reminds me that those guys didn't get any adulation, no appreciation. Our fans that were loyal, they were great to those guys. But the city? No. The school would never let me, but if it was up to me, I'd hang a banner for that team."

2006-07 Cincinnati Basketball Results

Nov. 10 at Fifth Third Arena – Cincinnati 70, Howard 39

Nov. 11 at Fifth Third Arena – Cincinnati 67, Tennessee-Martin 49

Nov. 12 at Fifth Third Arena – Cincinnati 63, High Point 51

Nov. 21 at Fifth Third Arena – Wofford 91, Cincinnati 90

Nov. 25 at Fifth Third Arena – Cincinnati 60, Central Michigan 50

Nov. 29 at Fifth Third Arena – Cincinnati 68, Oakland 61

Dec. 2 at Birmingham – UAB 59, Cincinnati 57

Dec. 9 at Atlantic City, N.J. – Cincinnati 80, Temple 71

Dec. 13 at Fifth Third Arena – Cincinnati 67, Xavier 57

Dec. 16 at Indianapolis – No. 4 Ohio State 72, Cincinnati 50

Dec. 23 at Fifth Third Arena – Cincinnati 80, North Carolina State 71

Dec. 27 at U.S. Bank Arena – Cincinnati 60, Miami (Ohio) 52

Dec. 30 at Cleveland – Ohio 79, Cincinnati 66

Jan. 4 at Memphis – No. 23 Memphis 88, Cincinnati 55

Jan. 7 at Fifth Third Arena – Rutgers 54, Cincinnati 42

Jan. 14 at Tampa – USF 74, Cincinnati 59

Jan. 17 at Syracuse. N.Y. – Syracuse 77, Cincinnati 76

Jan. 20 at Fifth Third Arena – Cincinnati 96, West Virginia 83 (OT)

Jan. 24 at Fifth Third Arena – No. 9 Pittsburgh 67, Cincinnati 51

Jan. 27 at Washington, D.C. – Georgetown 82, Cincinnati 67

Jan. 31 at Fifth Third Arena – Louisville 69, Cincinnati 63

Feb. 4 at Fifth Third Arena – St. John's 73, Cincinnati 64

Feb. 6 at Providence, R.I. – Providence 71, Cincinnati 70

Feb. 10 at Piscataway, N.J. – Rutgers 73, Cincinnati 69

Feb. 14 at Villanova, Pa. – Villanova 64, Cincinnati 48

Feb. 18 at Fifth Third Arena – Notre Dame 76, Cincinnati 64

Feb. 21 at Fifth Third Arena – No. 12 Georgetown 75, Cincinnati 65

Feb. 24 at Rosemont, Ill. – DePaul 58, Cincinnati 45

Feb. 28 at Fifth Third Arena – Cincinnati 70, Seton Hall 67 (OT)

March 3 at Morgantown, W.V. – West Virginia 79, Cincinnati 65

2006-07 Cincinnati Basketball Box Scores

Cincinnati 70, Howard 39
Nov. 10   Fifth Third Arena

HOWARD	FG	FT	TP	CINCINNATI	FG	FT	TP
Hudson	4	9	18	McGowan	5	0	10
Trotter	1	0	2	Williamson	7	4	18
Myatt	3	1	7	Sikes	2	3	9
Mitchell	0	3	3	Gentry	4	1	9
White	1	1	3	Warren	2	0	4
Mukole	1	0	2	Crowell	1	0	3
Gant	1	0	2	Vaughn	3	0	7
Kirkpatrick	1	0	2	Allen	4	2	10
				Lewis	0	1	1
TOTALS	12-56	13-17	39	TOTALS	28-68	10-19	70

3pt shots: 2-12 (Hudson 1-4, Myatt 1-2,   Mitchell 0-2, Hearn 0-1, White 1-2, Gant 0-1, Greene 0-1)

3pt shots: 4-15 (McGowan 0-1, Sikes 2-2, Gentry 0-3, Warren 0-2 Crowell 1-3, Vaughn 1-3, Allen 0-1)

Halftime: Cincinnati 35, Howard 17

Attendance: 7,608

Cincinnati 67, Tennessee-Martin 49
Nov. 11   Fifth Third Arena

TENN.-MARTIN					CINCINNATI			
	FG	FT	TP			FG	FT	TP
Lewis	2	0	4		McGowan	3	1	7
Woodford	2	1	5		Williamson	8	4	23
Knight	3	2	9		Sikes	6	3	18
Flatt	2	0	6		Gentry	3	0	7
Tolliver	4	3	12		Warren	1	3	5
Robinson	4	1	10		Vaughn	3	1	7
Jones	0	3	3					
TOTALS	17-54	10-20	49		TOTALS	24-59	12-21	67

3pt shots: 5-21 (Knight 1-4, Flatt 2-3, Tolliver 1-4, Robinson 1-6, Harris 0-1, Bailey 0-3)

3pt shots: 7-27 (McGowan 0-5, Williamson 3-5, Sikes 3-6, Gentry 1-4, Warren 0-2, Vaughn 0-4, Miller 0-1)

Halftime: Cincinnati 36, Tenn.-Martin 15

Attendance: 7,515

Cincinnati 63, High Point 51
Nov. 12   Fifth Third Arena

HIGH POINT	FG	FT	TP	CINCINNATI	FG	FT	TP
Reid	3	0	6	McGowan	5	3	13
Daniels	2	0	4	Williamson	3	0	8
Jefferson	6	0	15	Sikes	3	5	12
Quick	1	1	3	Gentry	1	0	3
Bowen	2	1	7	Warren	3	2	9
Crowder	2	0	5	Crowell	3	0	7
Harris	4	0	11	Vaughn	4	1	9
				Allen	1	0	2
TOTALS	20-59	2-5	51	TOTALS	23-55	11-19	63

3pt shots: 9-25 (Reid 0-3, Jefferson 3-9, Quick 0-1, Bowen 2-5, Crowder 1-2, Harris 3-5)

3pt shots: 6-17 (McGowan 0-2, Williamson 2-2, Sikes 1-2, Gentry 1-3, Warren 1-3, Crowell 1-2, Vaughn 0-1, Allen 0-2)

Halftime: Cincinnati 28, High Point 28

Attendance: 7,239

Wofford 91, Cincinnati 90
Nov. 21   Fifth Third Arena

WOFFORD	FG	FT	TP	CINCINNATI	FG	FT	TP
O'Connor	2	0	4	McGowan	1	0	2
Wheatley	3	1	7	Williamson	8	2	19
Nichols	6	4	20	Sikes	7	3	20
Estep	2	3	7	Gentry	5	0	13
Marshall	8	7	27	Vaughn	12	0	33
Salters	3	5	14	Crowell	1	1	3
Nixon	1	0	2				
Godzinski	3	1	8				
Lebelo	0	2	2				
TOTALS	28-53	23-29	91	TOTALS	34-63	5-8	90

3pt shots: 12-24 (O'Connor 0-2, Nichols 4-4, Estep 0-1, Marshall 4-5, Salters 3-6, Nixon 0-2, Sheehan 0-1, Godzinski 1-3)

3pt shots: 17-32 (McGowan 0-2, Williamson 1-1, Sikes 3-4, Gentry 3-6, Vaughn 9-17, Crowell 1-1, Warren 1-1)

Halftime: Cincinnati 42, Wofford 38

Attendance: 8,785

Cincinnati 60, Central Michigan 50
Nov. 25   Fifth Third Arena

CENTRAL MICHIGAN	FG	FT	TP		CINCINNATI	FG	FT	TP
Barrett	0	3	3		McGowan	3	6	12
Kellerman	1	0	3		Williamson	3	4	11
Spica	1	0	2		Sikes	1	3	5
Spencer	2	0	4		Gentry	2	0	5
Watson	8	5	23		Vaughn	8	0	19
Walters	1	0	2		Crowell	1	0	3
Bitze	1	2	5		Miller	1	0	3
Blevins	3	2	8		Allen	0	2	2

TOTALS   17-49 12-13 50   TOTALS   19-40 15-19 60

3pt shots: 4-19 (Barrett 0-1, Kellerman 1-4, Spencer 0-1, Watson 2-6, Bitze 1-6, Smyth 0-1)

3pt shots: 7-12 (McGowan 0-1, Williamson 1-1, Gentry 1-2, Vaughn 3-4, Crowell 1-1, Miller 1-1, Allen 0-1, Warren 0-1)

Halftime: Cincinnati 31, Central Michigan 22

Attendance: 7,589

Cincinnati 68, Oakland 61
Nov. 29   Fifth Third Arena

OAKLAND	FG	FT	TP	CINCINNATI	FG	FT	TP
Severovas	2	1	5	McGowan	3	3	9
Hopes	7	3	17	Williamson	11	4	27
Jones	5	2	14	Sikes	0	1	1
Billings	4	0	8	Vaughn	5	6	17
Kangas	1	0	3	Warren	6	0	12
Nelson	2	0	4	Allen	1	0	2
Cassise	2	2	8				
McCloskey	0	2	2				
TOTALS	23-58	10-13	61	TOTALS	26-58	14-18	68

3pt shots: 5-13 (Jones 2-3, Kangas 1-5, Cassise 2-5)

3pt shots: 2-13 (McGowan 0-1, Williamson 1-2, Sikes 0-1, Vaughn 1-5, Warren 0-1, Gentry 0-2, Crowell 0-1)

Halftime: Oakland 33, Cincinnati 29

Attendance: 7,351

UAB 59, Cincinnati 57
Dec. 2   Fifth Third Arena

UAB	FG	FT	TP
Holmes	3	0	6
Kinnard	5	0	12
Delaney	7	6	22
Mukubu	5	4	19
TOTALS	20-47	10-11	59

CINCINNATI	FG	FT	TP
McGowan	7	2	17
Williamson	2	1	5
Vaughn	6	0	16
Warren	4	0	9
Gentry	3	1	7
Allen	1	0	3
TOTALS	23-57	4-8	57

3pt shots: 9-20 (Kinnard 2-7, Delaney 2-4, Mukubu 5-5, White 0-1, Dortch 0-2, Mayfield 0-1)

3pt shots: 7-23 (McGowan 1-3, Williamson 0-1, Sikes 0-3. Vaughn 4-9, Warren 1-4, Gentry 0-1, Crowell 0-1, Allen 1-1)

Halftime: UAB 29, Cincinnati 23

Attendance 8,099

Cincinnati 80, Temple 71
Dec. 9   Atlantic City, N.J.

CINCINNATI	FG	FT	TP		TEMPLE	FG	FT	TP
McGowan	4	3	11		Dacons	4	2	10
Williamson	6	3	15		Olmos	1	1	3
Sikes	4	7	17		Salisbery	7	2	18
Vaughn	4	7	17		Inge	5	6	17
Warren	7	0	16		Christmas	5	9	20
Gentry	1	0	2		Kirkendoll	1	0	3
Barwin	1	0	2					

TOTALS   27-62 20-26 80   TOTALS   23-50 20-27 71

3pt shots: 6-22 (McGowan 0-2, Williamson 0-2, Sikes 2-4, Vaughn 2-6, Warren 2-5, Gentry 0-2, Allen 0-1)

3pt shots: 5-19 (Dacons 0-2, Salisbery 2-6, Inge 1-2, Christmas 1-3, Clark 0-3, Brooks 0-1, Kirkendoll 1-3)

Halftime: Temple 46, Cincinnati 39

Attendance: 4,307

Cincinnati 67, Xavier 57
Dec. 13   Fifth Third Arena

XAVIER	FG	FT	TP	**CINCINNATI**	FG	FT	TP
Duncan	4	4	14	McGowan	2	2	8
Cage	5	3	14	Williamson	6	4	18
Doellman	2	0	4	Sikes	1	1	3
Lavender	2	0	5	Vaughn	9	4	24
Burrll	0	0	0	Warren	3	6	12
Brown	3	2	8	Gentry	0	2	2
Raymond	2	0	6				
Cole	3	0	6				
TOTALS	21-50	9-14	57	TOTALS	21-60	19-26	67

3pt shots: 6-25 (Duncan 2-3, Cage 1-4, Lavender 1-6, Raymond 2-4, Burrell 0-4, Doellman 0-2, Graves 0-1, Brown 0-1)

3pt shots: 6-25 (McGowan 2-5, Williamson 2-5, Vaughn 2-10, Sikes 0-2, Warren 0-2, Gentry 0-1)

Halftime: Cincinnati 32, Xavier 29

Attendance: 13,176.

No. 4 Ohio State 72, Cincinnati 50
Dec. 16   Indianapolis

OHIO STATE	FG	FT	TP		CINCINNATI	FG	FT	TP
Harris	5	0	13		McGowan	0	2	2
Oden	6	2	14		Williamson	7	3	17
Conley	3	2	8		Sikes	1	3	5
Lewis	2	5	10		Vaughn	2	1	5
Butler	1	0	3		Warren	6	1	13
Lighty	0	6	6		Barwin	1	0	2
Cook	4	0	9		Miller	2	0	6
Terwilliger	1	1	3					
Hunter	3	0	6					

TOTALS 25-58, 16-23 72.

TOTALS 19-73, 10-16, 50

3pt shots: 6-23 (Harris 3-5, Conley 0-2, Lewis 1-6, Butler 1-5, Lighty 0-1, Cook 1-4).

3pt shots: 2-24 (McGowan 0-2, Williamson 0-3, Sikes 0-3, Vaughn 0-4, Warren 0-5, Gentry 0-1, Crowell 0-1, Barwin 0-1, Miller 2-2, Allen 0-2).

Halftime: Ohio State 42, Cincinnati 14

Attendance 18,356

Cincinnati 80, North Carolina State 71
Dec. 23   Fifth Third Arena

N. CAROLINA STATE	FG	FT	TP	CINCINNATI	FG	FT	TP
Horner	3	2	10	McGowan	6	3	15
Costner	6	1	14	Williamson	6	1	13
McCauley	9	4	22	Sikes	4	2	10
Fells	6	0	13	Vaughn	10	1	25
Grant	3	0	6	Warren	3	2	9
Ferguson	2	0	6	Gentry	0	1	1
				Crowell	0	3	3
				Miller	1	0	2
				Allen	1	0	2
TOTALS	29-51	7-15	71	TOTALS	31-69	13-17	80

3pt shots: 6-13 (Horner 2-3, Costner 1-2, Fells 1-4, Grant 0-1, Ferguson 2-3)

3pt shots: 0-2, Sikes 0-2, Vaughn 4-10, Warren 1-2, Gentry 0-1, Allen 0-2)

Halftime: North Carolina State 33, Cincinnati 30

Attendance: 9,549

Cincinnati 60, Miami (Ohio) 52
Dec. 27   U.S. Bank Arena

MIAMI	FG	FT	TP	CINCINNATI	FG	FT	TP
Peavey	9	4	22	McGowan	3	0	6
T. Politz	1	1	3	Williamson	3	0	6
Dierkers	2	1	5	Sikes	5	4	15
Penno	0	2	2	Vaughn	2	2	6
Moosmann	2	2	8	Warren	6	3	15
E. Politz	1	0	3	Gentry	4	0	8
Bramos	3	2	9	Crowell	1	0	2
				Barwin	1	0	2
TOTALS	18-46	12-17	52	TOTALS	25-52	9-14	60

3pt shot: 4-18 (Peavey 0-2, T. Politz
0-1, Penno 0-6, Moosmann 2-3,
E. Politz 1-2, Bramos 1-2, St. Clair 0-2)

3pt shots: 1-7 (Sikes 1-2, Vaughn 0-2,
Warren 0-1, Gentry 0-1, Crowell 0-1)

Halftime: Cincinnati 31, Miami 22

Attendance: 9,256

Ohio 79, Cincinnati 66
Dec. 30   Cleveland

CINCINNATI	FG	FT	TP		OHIO	FG	FT	TP
McGowan	6	0	13		Troutman	2	5	9
Williamson	7	1	15		Tillman	4	5	13
Sikes	2	2	6		Williams	4	12	20
Vaughn	2	0	4		Walther	5	4	18
Warren	7	0	15		Davis	6	2	15
Gentry	2	9	13		Chatman	1	2	4

TOTALS   26-55 12-15 66   TOTALS   22-52 30-36 79

3pt shot: 2-15 (McGowan 1-1, Sikes 0-1, Vaughn 0-4, Warren 1-6, Gentry 0-3)

3pt shot: 5-20 (Troutman 0-3, Walther 4-11, Davis 1-3, Van Kempen 0-1, King 0-2)

Halftime: Ohio 37, Cincinnati 26

Attendance: 3,437

No. 22 Memphis 88, Cincinnati 55

Jan. 4   Memphis

CINCINNATI	FG	FT	TP	MEMPHIS	FG	FT	TP
McGowan	7	4	20	Dozier	5	3	13
Williamson	4	3	11	Dorsey	3	0	6
Sikes	2	0	6	Kemp	7	1	21
Vaughn	3	1	8	Anderson	2	2	6
Warren	3	0	6	Roberts-Douglas	3	0	6
Gentry	1	0	2	Willis	1	0	2
Crowell	1	0	2	Niles	1	0	2
				Hunt	7	4	24
				Allen	1	1	3
				Mack	2	1	5
TOTALS	21-56	8-13	55	TOTALS	32-54	12-18	88

3pt shots: 5-13 (McGowan 2-2, Williamson 0-1, Sikes 2-5, Vaughn 1-2, Warren 0-1, Gentry 0-1, Crowell 0-1)

3pt shots: 12-28 (Kemp 6-9, Anderson 0-1, Roberts-Douglas 0-2, Willis 0-1, Hunt 6-7, Allen 0-3, Mack 0-4, Kooper 0-1)

Halftime: Memphis 54, Cincinnati 23

Attendance: 16,223

Rutgers 54, Cincinnati 42
Jan. 7   Fifth Third Arena

RUTGERS	FG	FT	TP	CINCINNATI	FG	FT	TP
Hill	4	5	13	McGowan	2	1	5
Inman	3	0	8	Williamson	2	2	6
Griffin	5	1	13	Sikes	7	0	17
Webb	4	1	13	Vaughn	1	0	2
Farmer	2	1	5	Warren	3	1	7
Bailey	1	0	2	Gentry	1	0	3
				Barwin	1	0	2
TOTALS	19-47	8-15	54	TOTALS	17-49	4-6	42

3pt shots: 8-16 (Inman 2-4, Griffin 2-5, Webb 4-4, Farmer 0-1, Nelson 0-2)

3pt shots: 4-21 (McGowan 0-1, Williamson 0-1, Sikes 3-5, Vaughn 0-7, Warren 0-2, Gentry 1-3, Crowell 0-1, Miller 0-1)

Halftime: Rutgers 21, Cincinnati 20

Attendance: 8,212

USF 74, Cincinnati 59
Jan. 14   Tampa

CINCINNATI	FG	FT	TP
McGowan	2	0	4
Williamson	1	0	2
Sikes	1	1	4
Vaughn	7	4	21
Warren	6	2	14
Gentry	3	0	8
Crowell	1	1	4
Barwin	1	0	2
TOTALS	22-66	8-16	59

3pt shots: 7-30 (McGowan 0-3, Sikes 1-2, Vaughn 3-16, Warren 0-2, Gentry 2-5, Crowell 1-2)

USF	FG	FT	TP
Buckley	4	6	16
Mattis	8	1	17
Gransberry	8	5	21
Bozeman	2	4	10
Howard	2	4	8
Saaka	0	2	2
TOTALS	24-50	22-35	74

3pt shots: 4-12 (Buckley 2-5, Bozeman 2-5, Howard 0-2)

Halftime: USF 35, Cincinnati 24

Attendance: 3,449

Syracuse 77, Cincinnati 76
Jan. 17   Syracuse, N.Y.

CINCINNATI	FG	FT	TP	RUTGERS	FG	FT	TP
McGowan	4	2	10	Roberts	7	3	17
Williamson	4	3	11	Nichols	7	4	22
Sikes	8	0	24	Rautins	2	0	5
Vaughn	5	1	13	Wright	3	1	8
Warren	2	0	5	Harris	0	2	2
Gentry	4	1	11	Devendorf	4	7	17
Allen	1	0	2	Gorman	2	0	6
TOTALS	28-77	7-11	76	TOTALS	25-49	17-21	77

3pt shots: 13-32 (McGowan 0-1, Sikes 8-12, Vaughn 2-10, Warren 1-5, Gentry 2-4)

3pt shots: 10-23 (Nichols 4-9, Rautins 1-4, Wright 1-3, Devendorf 2-4, Gorman 2-3)

Halftime: Syracuse 48, Cincinnati 34

Attendance: 22,248

Cincinnati 96, West Virginia 83 (OT)
Jan. 20   Fifth Third Arena

WEST VIRGINIA	FG	FT	TP	CINCINNATI	FG	FT	TP
Alexander	3	0	9	McGowan	3	2	9
Young	5	0	13	Williamson	6	5	17
Summers	3	3	9	Sikes	2	5	10
Nichols	1	2	4	Vaughn	4	2	12
Ruoff	5	7	21	Warren	5	6	16
Butler	4	4	14	Gentry	9	9	32
Mazzula	1	0	3				
Smith	1	0	2				
Smalligan	3	0	8				
TOTALS	26-61	16-19	83	TOTALS	29-64	29-41	96

3pt shots: 15-40 (Alexander 3-5, Young 3-12, Nichols 0-2, Ruoff 4-11, Butler 2-4, Mazzulla 1-2, Smith 0-1, Smalligan 2-3)

3pt shots: 9-20 (McGowan 1-3, Williamson 0-1, Sikes 1-4, Vaughn 2-5, Gentry 5-7)

Halftime: West Virginia 43, Cincinnati 31

End of regulation Cincinnati 75, West Virginia 75

Attendance: 9,390.

No. 9 Pittsburgh 67, Cincinnati 51
Jan. 24   Fifth Third Arena

PITTSBURG	FG	FT	TP		CINCINNATI	FG	FT	TP
Cook	4	0	9		McGowan	3	0	6
Gray	3	3	9		Williamson	6	3	15
Fields	6	0	18		Sikes	3	2	10
Graves	2	3	8		Vaughn	5	1	13
Benjamin	1	0	2		Warren	1	2	4
Ramon	3	1	10		Gentry	1	1	3
Biggs	0	1	1					
Young	4	1	10					
TOTALS	23-38	9-15	67		TOTALS	19-52	9-15	51

3pt shots: 12-19 (Kendall 0-1, Cook 1-1, Fields 6-7, Graves 1-3, Benjamin 0-2, Ramon 3-4, Young 1-1)

3pt shots: 4-18 (McGowan 0-1, Williamson 0-1, Sikes 2-4, Vaughn 2-8, Warren 0-3, Gentry 0-1)

Halftime: Pittsburgh 38, Cincinnati 26

Attendance: 9,196

Georgetown 82, Cincinnati 67
Jan. 27   Washington, D.C.

CINCINNATI	FG	FT	TP	GEORGETOWN	FG	FT	TP
McGowan	2	0	4	Green	6	3	17
Williamson	0	3	3	Summers	0	4	4
Sikes	7	0	19	Hibbert	11	4	26
Vaughn	5	4	18	Sapp	4	2	10
Warren	2	0	5	Wallace	2	7	13
Gentry	6	0	15	Macklin	2	0	4
Crowell	1	0	3	Ewing Jr.	3	0	8

TOTALS   23-47 7-8 67   TOTALS 28-58 20-26 82

3pt shots: 14-24 (McGowan 0-1,
Sikes 5-5, Vaughn 4-9, Warren 1-1,
Gentry 3-7, Crowell 1-1)

3pt shots: 6-18 (Green 2-3, Summers
0-3, Sapp 0-4, Wallace 2-4, Rivers 0-2,
Ewing Jr. 2-2)

Halftime: Georgetown 40, Cincinnati 35

Attendance: 13,106

Louisville 69, Cincinnati 53
Jan. 31   Fifth Third Arena

LOUISVILLE	FG	FT	TP	CINCINNATI	FG	FT	TP
Williams	3	5	13	McGowan	1	2	4
Palacios	4	4	13	Williamson	0	0	0
Padgett	8	2	18	Sikes	3	3	9
Sosa	3	1	7	Vaughn	6	4	18
Jenkins	2	2	8	Gentry	9	1	22
Scott	1	0	2				
McGee	0	2	2				
Smith	2	0	6				
TOTALS	23-51	16-18	69	TOTALS	19-62	10-17	53

3pt shots: 7-22 (Williams 2-6, Palacios 1-2, Sosa 0-5, Jenkins 2-4, McGee 0-2, Smith 2-3).

3pt shots: 5-24 (Sikes 0-3, Vaughn 2-8, Gentry 3-8, Crowell 0-3, Miller 0-1, Allen 0-1)

Halftime: Louisville 33, Cincinnati 19

Attendance 10,881

St. John's 73, Cincinnati 64
Feb. 4   Fifth Third Arena

ST. JOHN'S	FG	FT	TP	CINCINNATI	FG	FT	TP
Calhoun	5	7	18	McGowan	1	1	3
Mason	3	2	9	Williamson	5	3	13
Hamilton	4	7	15	Sikes	5	3	15
Lawrence	3	1	9	Vaughn	5	2	17
Patterson	3	1	10	Warren	2	5	9
Wright	0	6	6	Gentry	2	2	7
Spears	2	2	6				
TOTALS	20-41	26-32	73	TOTALS	20-60	16-27	64

3pt shots 7-15 (Calhoun 1-2, Mason 1-1, Hamilton 0-1, Lawrence 2-2, Patterson 3-6, Wright 0-2, Torres 0-1)

3pt shots: 8-30 (Sikes 2-8, Vaughn 5-14, Warren 0-3, Gentry 1-5)

Halftime: St. John's 30, Cincinnati 24

Attendance: 7,902

Providence 71, Cincinnati 70
Feb. 6   Providence, R.I.

CINCINNATI	FG	FT	TP	PROVIDENCE	FG	FT	TP
Williamson	7	1	15	McDermott	4	0	10
Sikes	4	1	11	Kale	0	2	2
Gentry	3	0	8	Hill	7	2	16
Vaughn	5	0	14	Curry	8	3	24
Warren	5	1	11	Efejuku	5	0	13
Crowell	0	1	1	Williams	1	0	3
Barwin	2	0	4	McKenzie	1	0	3
McGowan	3	0	6				
TOTALS	29-58	4-14	70	TOTALS	26-47	7-9	71

3pt shots: 8-20 (Sikes 2-4, Gentry 2-3, Vaughn 4-10, Warren 0-3)

3pt shots: (12-27 (McDermott 2-3, Curry 5-8, Efejuku 3-8, Williams 1-4, McKenzie 1-4)

Halftime: Providence 38, Cincinnati 38

Attendance: 8,557

Rutgers 73, Cincinnati 69
Feb. 10   Piscataway, N.J.

CINCINNATI	FG	FT	TP	RUTGERS	FG	FT	TP
Williamson	7	5	19	Hill	6	6	18
Sikes	3	1	7	Inman	3	3	10
Gentry	3	0	9	Griffin	4	4	14
Vaughn	7	0	18	Webb	3	5	11
Warren	6	1	13	Farmer	1	4	7
McGowan	1	1	3	Nelson	2	0	5
				N'Diaye	2	2	6
				Bailey	0	2	2
TOTALS	27-57	7-10	69	TOTALS	21-41	26-30	73

3pt shots: 8-17 (Sikes 0-5, Gentry 3-4, Vaughn 4-5, Warren 0-2, 1-1)

3pt shots: 5-11 (Inman 1-2, Griffin 2-3, Webb 0-3, Farmer 1-2, McGowan Nelson 1-1)

Halftime: Rutgers 39, Cincinnati 29

Attendance: 7,104

Villanova 64, Cincinnati 48
Feb. 14   Villanova, P.A.

CINCINNATI	FG	FT	TP	VILLANOVA	FG	FT	TP
Williamson	4	6	15	Clark	2	0	5
Sikes	2	0	6	Sumpter	3	0	8
Gentry	0	3	3	Sheridan	4	0	8
Vaughn	1	2	4	Reynolds	2	4	9
Warren	2	3	7	Nardi	5	2	16
Crowell	1	0	2	Benn	2	1	5
Barwin	1	2	4	Redding	1	0	2
Miller	1	0	3	Cunningham	3	5	11
McGowan	1	2	4				
TOTALS	13-38	18-22	48	TOTALS	22-55	12-13	64

3pt shots: 4-14 (Williamson 1-2, Sikes 2-4, Gentry 0-3, Vaughn 0-1, Miller 1-3, Crowell 0-1)

3pt shots: 8-20 (Clark 1-5, Sumpter 2-3, Reynolds 1-5, , Nardi 4-5, Redding 0-1, Anderson 0-1)

Halftime: Villanova 34, Cincinnati 17

Attendance: 6,500

Notre Dame 76, Cincinnati 64
Feb. 18   Fifth Third Arena

NOTRE DAME	FG	FT	TP	CINCINNATI	FG	FT	TP
Kurz	1	3	5	Williamson	8	7	23
Harangody	5	1	11	Sikes	1	0	3
Jackson	3	2	10	Vaughn	8	4	22
Falls	6	6	23	Warren	2	1	5
Carter	1	0	3	Crowell	1	0	2
Peoples	2	0	5	Barwin	1	0	3
Hillesland	3	1	7	McGowan	3	0	7
Ayers	4	0	12				
TOTALS	25-48	13-17	76	TOTALS	23-58	13-18	64

3pt shots: 13-20 (Jackson 2-4, Falls 5-8, Carter 1-3, Peoples 1-1, Ayers 4-4)

3pt shots: 5-18 (Williamson 0-1, Sikes 1-2, Gentry 0-2, Vaughn 2-9, Warren 0-1, Crowell 0-1, Barwin 1-2, McGowan 1-1)

Halftime: Notre Dame 37, Cincinnati 30

Attendance: 11,038

No. 12 Georgetown 75, Cincinnati 65
Feb. 21   Fifth Third Arena

GEORGETOWN	FG	FT	TP	CINCINNATI	FG	FT	TP
Summers	2	2	6	Williamson	7	1	15
Green	6	7	21	Sikes	3	2	9
Hibbert	3	1	7	Gentry	2	0	6
Wallace	6	2	17	Crowell	2	0	5
Sapp	6	1	14	Vaughn	5	6	19
Macklin	1	0	2	Barwin	1	1	3
Rivers	2	0	6	McGowan	2	0	5
Ewing Jr.	0	2	2	Warren	1	1	3
TOTALS	26-48	15-21	75	TOTALS	23-58	11-18	65

3pt shots: 8-20 (Summers 0-4
Green 2-3, Wallace 3-6, Sapp 1-4,
Rivers 2-2 Ewing Jr. 0-1)

3pt shots: 8-23 (Sikes 1-3, Gentry 2-4,
Crowell 1-1, Vaughn 3-13, McGowan
1-2)

Halftime: Georgetown 37, Cincinnati 31

Attendance: 8,163

DePaul 58, Cincinnati 45
Feb. 24   Rosemont, Ill.

CINCINNATI	FG	FT	TP	DEPAUL	FG	FT	TP
Williamson	6	4	16	Chandler	6	1	14
Gentry	3	0	7	Thompson	1	0	2
Crowell	1	0	2	Burns	2	6	11
Vaughn	3	2	8	Mejia	3	2	9
Barwin	0	2	2	Clarke	2	0	5
McGowan	3	1	8	Clinkscales	1	0	2
Warren	1	0	2	Heard	3	1	7
				Walker	1	0	2
				Butler	2	2	6
TOTALS	17-51	9-12	45	TOTALS	21-58	12-18	58

3pt shots: 2-13 (Sikes 0-1, Gentry 1-5, Vaughn 0-5, McGowan 1-2)

3pt shots: 4-19 (Chandler 1-4, Burns 1-4, Mejia 1-3, Clarke 1-4, Clinkscales 0-1, Moses 0-1, Heard 0-1, Walker 0-1)

Halftime DePaul 35, Cincinnati 20

Attendance: 10,651

Cincinnati 70, Seton Hall 67 (OT)
Feb. 28   Fifth Third Arena

SETON HALL	FG	FT	TP	CINCINNATI	FG	FT	TP
Laing	8	2	18	Allen	1	0	3
Garcia	3	0	6	McGowan	3	2	8
Nutter	3	2	10	Williamson	6	4	16
Harvey	8	5	24	Vaughn	5	8	20
Gause	2	0	6	Warren	4	4	13
Davis	1	0	3	Sikes	3	0	7
				Barwin	1	1	3
TOTALS	25-66	9-16	67	TOTALS	23-58	19-28	70

3pt shots: 8-22 (Laing 0-2, Nutter 2-6, Harvey 3-5, Gause 2-5, Davis 1-4)

3pt shots: 5-17 (Allen 1-1, McGowan 0-3, Vaughn 2-6, Warren 1-1, Sikes 1-4, Miller 0-2)

Halftime Cincinnati 31, Seton Hall 24

End of regulation Cincinnati 59, Seton Hall 59

Attendance 8,109

West Virginia 79, Cincinnati 65
March 3   Morgantown, W.V.

CINCINNATI	FG	FT	TP
McGowan	6	4	16
Williamson	7	0	14
Sikes	2	1	7
Vaughn	7	3	18
Warren	1	0	2
Crowell	1	0	3
Miller	2	0	5
TOTALS	26-57	8-1	65

WEST VIRIGNIA	FG	FT	TP
Alexander	2	3	8
Young	4	3	12
Summers	2	1	5
Nichols	2	10	16
Ruoff	9	0	23
Butler	2	0	6
Mazzulla	1	0	3
Smalligan	2	0	6
TOTALS	24-49	17-21	79

3pt shots: 5-17 (McGowan 0-1, Sikes 2-3, Vaughn 1-9, Warren 0-1, Crowell 1-2, Miller 1-1)

3pt shots: 14-28 (Alexander 1-2, Young 1-6, Summers 0-1, Nichols 2-5, Ruoff 5-8, Butler 2-3, Mazzulla 1-1, Smalligan 2-2)

Halftime: West Virginia 40, Cincinnati 25

Attendance: 11,968

Records

All games	Conference games	Non-conference
11-19 overall	2-14 overall	9-5 overall
10-8 home	2-6 home	8-2 home
0-9 away	0-8 away	0-1 away
1-2 neutral	0-0 neutral	1-2 neutral

Team Statistics

	Cincinnati	Opponents
Scoring	64.6	67.7
Field Goal Percentage	40.5	44.5
3-PT Field Goal Percentage	30.8	37.7
Free Throw Percentage	66.1	73.8
Rebounds	33.6	33.3
Assists	12.5	13.1
Turnovers	12.7	15.0
Steals	7.7	5.1
Blocks	1.9	4.2
Attendance	8,831/158,966	11,090/125,906

2006-07 Season Statistics

Player	GP-GS	Min.	FG-FGA	PCT	3FG-FGA	PCT	FT-FTA	PCT	REB	ASST	PTS	AVG
Vaughn	30-27	33.0	152-407	37.3	63-216	29.2	67-89	75.3	3.4	106	434	14.5
Williamson	30-30	30.9	157-322	48.8	11-31	35.5	81-139	58.3	7.3	31	406	13.5
Sikes	30-29	29.3	92-228	40.4	45-106	42.5	56-84	66.7	5.0	41	285	9.5
McGowan	30-24	28.4	95-214	44.4	11-49	22.4	46-61	75.4	5.1	29	247	8.2
Warren	30-26	29.2	94-250	37.6	9-60	15.0	44-73	60.3	3.7	97	241	8.0
Gentry	28-11	25.7	72-200	36.0	31-92	33.7	31-42	73.8	2.8	35	206	7.4
Crowell	30-2	9.7	16-42	38.1	9-25	36.0	5-8	62.5	0.8	25	46	1.5
Allen	20-1	6.8	10-31	32.3	2-12	16.7	4-5	80.0	1.1	2	26	1.3
Barwin	23-0	10.3	10-23	43.5	0-1	00.0	7-13	53.8	1.4	5	27	1.2
Miller	25-0	5.6	7-22	31.8	5-12	41.7	0-2	0.0	0.8	5	19	0.8
Lewis	1-0	1.0	0-0	0.0	0-0	0.0	0-0	0.0	0.0	0	0	0
Total	30	—	705-1739	40.5	186-604	30.8	342-516	66.1	33.6	376	1937	64.6
Opp.	30	—	685-1539	44.5	231-612	37.7	431-584	73.8	33.3	393	2032	67.7

ABOUT THE AUTHOR

Bill Koch is a Cincinnati native and UC graduate. During his career as a Cincinnati sports writer, he has primarily covered UC athletics, but has also been the featured columnist at The Cincinnati Post. He has covered preps, was the beat writer for Xavier basketball for three years, and has written extensively about the Reds and Major League Baseball. Koch is the author of five previous books: The Pride of Price Hill, Nothing Changes, I Can't Believe I Got Paid for This, Inside the Crosstown Shootout, and Best of the Bearcats.

Made in the USA
Columbia, SC
31 January 2019